THE
EXCITEMENT
IS BUILDING

Millard & Linda Fuller

THE EXCITEMENT IS BUILDING

WORD PUBLISHING

Dallas·London·Vancouver·Melbourne

Library of Congress Cataloging-in-Publication Data

Fuller, Millard, 1935–
    The excitement is building / Linda and Millard Fuller.
       p.   cm.
    ISBN 0-8499-3209-2 (pbk.)
    1. Habitat for Humanity International, Inc. 2. Poor—Housing—United States. I. Fuller, Linda, 1941– . II. Title.
    HD7287.96.U6F85   1990
    363.5'83—dc20   90–32949
                                          CIP

Printed in the United States of America
0 1 2 3 4 9 RRD 9 8 7 6 5 4 3 2 1

This book is dedicated to our dear friends and Habitat co-workers David Rowe and Tom Hall who have been so very committed to the work of Habitat for Humanity for many years and whose dedication has contributed in countless ways to building the excitement in this unfolding saga of faith-activated house, community and people building.

—MILLARD AND LINDA FULLER

Contents

Foreword

This book, written by Millard and Linda Fuller, expresses the soul and spirit of Habitat for Humanity. It will be difficult for anyone to read it without shedding a few tears—not of sorrow, but of wonder and joy as the sentiments of volunteers and new Habitat homeowners are shared.

It will be obvious that the authors give me and Rosalynn much more attention and credit than we deserve. There are hundreds of people like the Fullers who devote their full time to building homes in partnership with God's people in need. We only serve as carpenters for one week a year, and give some help with publicity and fund-raising. Despite this comparatively small role, it is a true pleasure and very gratifying for us to be integral members of the Habitat family.

The excitement that comes across on almost every page of *The Excitement Is Building* is typical of the way Millard and Linda have lived and inspired others for almost fifteen years. They are the true heroes of Habitat. Often it has seemed to me that they were overly exuberant and naive as they began to explain their goals for the next project or the coming year. Walk 1200 miles! Increase next year's contributions tenfold! The Carter Work Camp build 203 homes in one week! At first inclined to calm them down to a more reasonable level of expectation, almost invariably we have become convinced enough to be equally naive and overly exuberant. In general, with faith and hard work, their dreams have been exceeded by later reality. This book explains why such modern day miracles are happening.

Jimmy Carter

A Word of Explanation and Acknowledgments

We collaborated totally in writing this book. The two of us are now telling this story *together*. When you read "we," "us" or "our" in the text this is usually us—Millard and Linda Fuller. Occasionally, these words will have a larger meaning, most likely Habitat for Humanity or a group of Habitat people, but that should be obvious from the context. When an event or experience was shared by only one of us, the third person is employed, i.e., "Millard said . . ." or "Linda explained . . . ," etc. Materials for this book were gathered from many sources, but especially from Habitat people working in projects all across North America and abroad and from Habitat Board members, Advisors, Regional Directors and staff. We express deepest thanks to all of these folks for their good help; and a special word of appreciation goes to all those people whose stories, information and pictures were not used. We tried to include all we could, but space limitations dictated that much had to be left out.

Most of the writing was done during the summer and fall of 1989 at "Glencove," a rustic lodge surrounded by gigantic white pines on Lake Rabun in North Georgia, "The Dogwood," a lovely lake home overlooking Robin Lake in southern Michigan, and at the home of Fred and Martha Lamar in Greencastle, Indiana. We want to voice our heartfelt gratitude to Chrys and John Street, owners of "Glencove," and to LeRoy and Phyllis Troyer, owners of "The Dogwood," for making these quiet retreats available to us and to Fred and Martha for allowing us to move in on them in October to write the final chapters of the rough draft. All of these caring people are not only cherished friends, they are dedicated Habitat partners. Chrys Street was the key person in founding Cobb County, Georgia, Habitat for Humanity, LeRoy Troyer is a member of the International Board of Habitat for Humanity and Fred Lamar is chaplain of DePauw University and has long been involved in sending DePauw students to work in Habitat projects in the U.S. and overseas.

From the bottom of our hearts, we thank Lynda Stephenson of Woodridge, Illinois, a talented writer and editor, who took our manuscript and molded it into a much better book. It would be impossible to give her too much credit for her enormous contribution to this publication.

We want to thank all of the people at Habitat headquarters in Americus who helped us with this book, but especially we want to express appreciation to:

• Doralee Robertson, director of our media department, for her *many* contributions to the book including making numerous, valuable changes in the manuscript, for coordinating the assembly of the appendices and being a real friend and great encourager in getting this book out!

• The entire media department for their help in getting the book ready for publication, but especially to Bob Lucas and Ray Scioscia for a lot of photographs and Mack Farquhar for finding specific pictures in our voluminous files; Craig Bunyea for preparing the maps; and Nick Compy and Phil Buchanan for copying (several times) the manuscript.

• Jim Purks, Rick Hathaway, Carol Pezzelli Wise and Karen Higgs for reading the manuscript and contributing good suggestions on how to make it flow more smoothly and for correcting some factual errors.

• David Macfarlane and Mary Ann Moore for ordering a word processor for Linda and training her to use it in typing the original manuscript.

• Sherry Weeks and RaeAnn Flick, Millard's secretaries, for their faithful typing of hundreds of letters associated with the book.

• All the great folks at Word Incorporated, with whom we enjoy the finest spirit of cooperation that could possibly exist between authors and a publisher.

All revenues, including royalties, from the sale of this book will go directly into the support of this growing ministry to build more houses and even more excitement. If this story builds your excitement, we hope you will share it with others who may want to become involved. Of course, we hope *you* will get personally involved, too, if you are not already.

—MILLARD AND LINDA FULLER

A Day in the Life of Habitat for Humanity

On a hot day in July, Bob Hope walked onto a Habitat construction site in Charlotte, North Carolina, picked up a hammer and drove a nail into a window frame. He bent it.

Nearby, former President Jimmy Carter, wearing a pair of old jeans, sneakers, and a heavy leather tool belt, was working on the same site with his wife Rosalynn, driving nails, sawing boards, putting in ceilings. . . .

Up and down the block, 350 volunteer workers were in high gear racing to complete fourteen Habitat homes that families would move into by week's end.

Across the country, in Sacramento, California, the Acosta family, who lived in a small rented one-bedroom upstairs apartment over a store, was working with a host of volunteers on a two-bedroom house with a fenced-in back yard.

On the other side of the world, in Malawi, Southern Africa, national radio and television were covering the dedication of two houses built by Habitat workers.

In Kasulu, Tanzania, five houses were being built and eight were dedicated with the help of 150 Tanzanian volunteers. Each volunteer worker was presented a Bible, and all the houses were toured by visitors.

In Boston, Chattanooga, Memphis, St. Petersburg, Detroit, Grand Rapids, Kansas City, Dallas, Denver, Atlanta, and many other places, the hammers were flying, almost in synchronization.

The sounds rang out across the country as thousands of volunteers were sawing, hammering, digging, laughing, crying, while hundreds of families also worked and forced themselves to believe that dreams do come true.

Add the hammers flying around the world—in India, Zaire, Peru, the Solomon Islands, Kenya, Costa Rica, Haiti, Nicaragua, Guatemala—and the Habitat racket was the kind that would be heard long after this day was over.

And for each house built there was a dedication service, like the one held at the end of the week in the small town of Randolph, Massachusetts. About seventy-five people crowded into the yard and poured into the street in front of Sharon Gilmore's home, which had recently been renovated by scores of Habitat volunteers working with Sharon and her three boys. Sharon stood to speak, but dissolved into tears. Her fourteen-year-old son Shawn took the microphone gently from her and said in a soft but steady voice, "Mama's not going to be able to say anything. I'll talk for the family. What you see here is a miracle. It is a miracle of love. We were suffering in this house with eleven leaks, no insulation—and no money to fix anything. Then you folks came to help us. We worked together and made a miracle."

That was the first Habitat House-Raising Week. We called it "blitz-building" and with the same excitement and deep feelings Sharon Gilmore and her sons expressed, we dubbed that summer "The Miracle Summer of 1987." Habitat crews had never built and renovated so many houses at one time before. And it changed the course of Habitat for Humanity. We were on our way to a new plateau. We caught a glimpse of our future, a future we are now living.

Let us tell you about some of the people who make days like the ones described above happen. Let us share the stories of the people who mark such days as miracles for their families. And let us document for you the amazing flood of growth and new directions this "crazy" idea of giving people a decent place to live has taken.

Walk with us on our marathon walks, build with us in far-off places, experience the transformations that a band of volunteers can produce for themselves and others, and be moved by the stories of changed lives.

We are so excited—and that *Excitement Is Building.*

I

Building
Excitement

1

The Excitement Is Building

On July 24, 1989, there was a mortgage-burning ceremony for Bo and Emma Johnson's house.

But this was no ordinary mortgage-burning. This was the mortgage on the very first home built by Koinonia's Partnership Housing Program, the forerunner of Habitat for Humanity.

In 1969 when Bo and Emma Johnson moved their children—Junior, Sally, Cookie, Queenie, and Baby Sister—from their unpainted, uninsulated shack without plumbing into a simple, concrete block house with a modern kitchen, an indoor bathroom, a good heating system, and a large, beautifully landscaped yard, the sale price was $6,000 for the thousand-square-foot house, to be repaid at $25 a month for twenty years, with no interest.

Every month over the next twenty years Bo and Emma made their monthly payments until, finally, they paid that last one—six months ahead of schedule. It was the very first house of the Koinonia program to be paid off by its owners.

We were part of Koinonia Farm in 1969. Millard was the director of this Christian community, located in southwest Georgia near Americus. On that November day when Millard helped carry Bo and Emma's furniture across Georgia Highway 49 to their new house and a new life, the idea for hundreds of more such houses for other needy families was only a distant and dim possibility. But by that mortgage-burning day in 1989 there were 457 Habitat projects in twenty-nine nations. Over 5,000 houses in all had been built around the world and new ones were going up at the rate of half a dozen a day.

Their Success Story Is Ours

And so Bo and Emma's success story is also that of Habitat for Humanity. Like so many of their neighbors, Bo and Emma were poor. They were also largely uneducated and landless, descendants of the slaves who once populated the surrounding farmlands. There was no way they, and others like them, could go into town and get a loan from a bank to build a house. Only a unique program, taking into consideration the limited resources and income of people like Bo and Emma, could meet their need for housing on terms they could afford to pay.

Clarence Jordan (famous for his "Cotton Patch" versions of the New Testament) with his wife Florence and Martin and Mabel England founded Koinonia Farm in 1942. He understood the plight of his poor neighbors.[1] He also knew God's plan for solving the problem. The Bible teaches that profit should not be made on the backs of the poor. Specifically, no interest should be charged when lending money to them.

That was the beginning. But it took a long time for the ideas to take on literal concrete form.

In 1965, we had left a successful business in Montgomery, Alabama, and all the trappings of an affluent lifestyle and had struck out on a new life of Christian service. With our children Chris and Kim, we visited Koinonia Farm for a month late that year. Then we served in other ministries for a couple of years. (See earlier books for more information on that period.[2]) In 1968, a group of us along with Clarence launched a new ministry at Koinonia which we called Koinonia Partners. Partnership Housing was a vital component of the new work. And it was this program which built Bo and Emma's house and many more. For nearly five years we lived and worked at Koinonia Farm, steadily building houses.[3]

Then in early 1973 our family, now increased by two with the birth of daughters Faith and Georgia, moved to Zaire in Central Africa where we launched a housing project in cooperation with the Church of Christ of Zaire. When we arrived back at

Koinonia in August 1976, a group of twenty-six people from all over the United States met at Koinonia to form a new organization to continue the work pioneered at Koinonia and in Zaire, an organization to be named "Habitat for Humanity." This was the idea: Each local Habitat project to be formed would be totally ecumenical, each would keep the overhead as low as possible and would be financed by a revolving Fund for Humanity. Money would be raised from private sources—individuals, churches, companies, etc. Volunteers would do most of the building to keep the cost down and to give people an opportunity to do "hands on" work as an expression of their faith. Houses would always be simple, but they would be solid and of quality construction. They would be sold to needy families with no profit added and no interest charged. And the families would be involved through "sweat equity." They would be required to give several hundred hours of work toward building their own houses and houses for others.

After twenty years, Bo and Emma's house is beautiful still, with the lawn neatly mowed and the house freshly painted. And their story is a testament to what the power of a decent place to live and shared love can do in a family, especially for the children. One of their children is a lawyer, another, a psychologist, and still another, a nurse. Each child, in his or her own way, is making a positive contribution to the world.

Small Flame/Large Flame

An editorial in the *Atlanta Constitution* captioned, "A Nice Little Case of Arson," compared the small flame of the mortgage-burning to the larger flame of Habitat for Humanity, how it is growing ever brighter across the land and world.

No More Shacks!, published in 1986, along with our earlier books, tells the full story in detail—the beginning and the burgeoning hope of Habitat. What's been happening since its publication, though, is the hope becoming fulfilled—the story of this book.

And the story is almost too exciting to believe.

We have walked nearly 3,000 miles, spread the vision around the globe, and Habitat for Humanity has become more and more a household name across the United States and Canada. By the beginning of the 1990s, houses were going up in more than 500 cities, towns, and villages in thirty nations. Ten houses a day. Soon to be twelve. Then, fifteen. Twenty. And work will be going on in a thousand cities by 1994. We're aiming for 2,000 cities by the year 2000!

The Excitement *IS* Building—and it's building because people have responded to this "crazy" idea and have volunteered by the thousands to make it happen. So much has happened so quickly.

You read of one of the most action-packed days of Habitat history in the Prologue—"A Day in the Life of Habitat," a day in 1987. It was part of three of the most exhilarating years we could ever have imagined. In the summer of 1986, we led a Walk to Kansas City, in the summer of 1987 we joined thousands of people who participated in making "House-Raising Week" a great success, and then that momentum rolled us right into the amazing summer of 1988 when everything was done—building houses and walking all at the same time. We can only give you the highlights of these "miracle" years, but we must share the excitement with you.

A Thousand Miles—1986

The week before July 30, 1986, walkers started arriving in Americus, Georgia, from across the North American continent and around the globe—from Costa Rica, Zaire, Papua New Guinea, Bolivia, India, Uganda, Peru, Germany, and Ireland. On the morning of the thirtieth, Jimmy and Rosalynn Carter drove over from Plains to walk the first nine miles with us, back to Plains.

Kansas City was a thousand miles and fifty days ahead of us. Over 600 people poured out of the Habitat headquarters parking lot into Church Street and with banners flying, we set out. The three purposes of the Walk were: 1) walk a thousand miles to Kansas City and raise a million dollars for the ministry of Habitat for Humanity; 2) raise consciousness about shelter so that more and more people would join us in our effort to eliminate poverty housing and homelessness; and 3) get all the walkers to Kansas City alive and well, with no injuries at all!

For the next seven weeks, we walked the thousand miles to Kansas City, battling 110-degree heat, thunderstorms, and swarms of gnats. We and our fellow walkers ate meals along the highway under huge trees, slept in churches and campgrounds and civic centers, drank free soft drinks donated by grocery stores, and ate home-cooked meals prepared by local organizations and churches. We marched in parades, were escorted by horseback riders, held rallies with local dignitaries and congressmen, nursed sore bodies and blistered feet, were serenaded by gospel choirs, showered mercifully with fire engine hoses, held a wedding, welcomed people who joined us at the spur of the moment, and—as you might imagine—made the kind of friends you keep for a lifetime.

The people we met were as colorful as the country is diverse. The vast majority seemed to catch the Habitat fever gladly.

For instance, in Sylacauga, Alabama, a young man named Anthony Watts saw all the commotion and asked what we were doing. He had not known about either Habitat or the Walk, but when he heard our story, he quickly packed his bag and joined us. He stayed with the Walk all the way to Kansas City and became our super salesman and fund-raiser along the way.

Seeing America at Walking Speed

We found ourselves viewing the countryside in a wonderful way you can never do while cruising along a highway in a car at fifty-five miles per hour. In the Arkansas Delta, for instance, with its totally flat land interlaced with canals and lush fields of rice, cotton and soybeans, we saw a lot of shacks, especially in the small towns and villages. We realized what we were fighting, but we also saw what a beautiful land and what willing people we had to work with.

All the arrangements for lodging, meals, police escorts, greetings, and proclamations by officials and church leaders were made by our advance team. These hard-working folks did a super job of having all arrangements made at every stop, day by day. Barbara Van Horn was one of them.[4] She felt a strong sense of God's hand in their work.

"There hasn't been a single day that I didn't have at least one moment when I was covered with goose bumps and filled with shivers about the way God had worked to arrange it to put the right people in the right places and put the whole thing together," she told us.

Churches of different denominations, people of different backgrounds, economic levels, and races joined together to help the Walk leave an impact on their communities as we all made our way through them.

Of course, there were long periods of quiet walking in between the towns and cities. That's when we'd get creative. A good example was Dave Enting's umbrella hat—a miniature umbrella mounted on top of a cap so it could be worn instead of carried. Linda jumped rope and led the walkers in a "bunny hop" or two to cut the boredom. All of us sang and sang, especially the song that's come to be an unofficial marching song for Habitat for Humanity, "We're Marching to Zion."

But there were also serious moments none of us can ever forget.

Like the day a delegation from Cartersville, Georgia, Habitat intercepted the Walk in Alabama where we had stopped to eat lunch. They arranged six chairs at the end of a tent and invited all the walkers to come up so they could wash our feet. And they not only washed and gently dried the feet of each walker, they also anointed them with soothing oil. All of us were greatly moved by this beautiful act of love and affirmation of what we were doing.

Or like the day there was a wedding. Two of our walkers, Fred Schippert and Ellen Olsen, had met some months back when both were volunteers at Habitat headquarters in Americus. During the Walk they had decided to get married. The day of the wedding, all the walkers gathered wild flowers along the road to decorate the church. The service was elegant in its simplicity, complete with flute and singing, and it was crowned by the Lord's Prayer, recited in segments in thirteen different languages.

("Habitaters" to the core, Fred and Ellen returned to his home in Detroit after the Walk to help bring into existence

Detroit Habitat for Humanity. Then, after training in Americus, they moved to Anahuac, Mexico, to work in the Habitat project there. We visited Fred and Ellen in Anahuac in late February 1990. The week following they moved to Mexico City to start the first Habitat project in that huge metropolis.)

Or the day a news helicopter from KYTV out of Springfield, Missouri, flew overhead, landed in a field beside the highway, interviewed us and then gave Linda a ride over the line of walkers to take photos.

And there isn't any way we could forget the night all the walkers were regaled by an orchestra in a downtown park in El Dorado Springs, Missouri. The next day we walked on to Nevada (Missouri, that is) and that evening went as a group to the local football stadium where the Friday night high school football game was in progress. During half time, our group marched around the field with our banners. Millard actually sat in the press box announcing about the walkers and what we all were doing.

We didn't always get a great reception. Dean DeBoer, at the head of the walkers, tried to talk the manager of a service station into allowing us to pause there for a few minutes as a rest stop. The manager responded angrily and told Dean to get off his property. Dean didn't argue. A large German Shepherd dog was chained nearby. And as we walked by, the dog barked viciously at every one of us, making his sentiments crystal clear.

Money Comes in Crazy Ways

At most of the rallies held nightly in the cities and towns we walked through, Millard would tell audiences about the worldwide work of Habitat and give the three purposes of the Walk. He would seek to inspire and motivate the crowd to join in the growing movement of Habitat for Humanity.

People would make contributions during the rallies. But that was by no means the only way money was raised. All along the Walk, people gave—on the road, at church services, at rest stops. Someone once threw a handful of dollar bills from the window of a car passing by. And walkers even found a lot of money along the road, mostly pennies, nickels, and dimes. (This "found" money was stored in a jar and auctioned off along with shoes and walking sticks and other such items at the end of the trip.)

Most of the money generated, though, was from pledges. People would pledge so much a mile for each walker. Then, after they had walked their miles, the people who had pledged would give the promised amount.

Norma Ueleke of Nashville, Tennessee, walked a total of 357 miles and received $4,000 from people who pledged for her walking. After the Walk, she sent a letter to all her contributors, beautifully reflecting on the deep meaning of the Walk for her and on the impact it had on all of us:

> A typical day would begin at 4:15 A.M. By 5:30, we had packed, eaten breakfast, and were on the road. Lunch would be about sixteen miles down the road followed by more walking until mid-afternoon. We then were taken where we were to spend the night— usually a church or high school. Once again we'd find our luggage, make up our bedrolls, and shower. Many evenings were spent at potluck suppers and services. Lights would go out at 10:00 P.M.

> While in training several persons gave me articles explaining the importance of drinking water during physical activity. I carried a canteen and drank water religiously. In our culture today where coffee, tea, and soft drinks have long since replaced water as a beverage, it is hard to grasp the significance of Christ comparing a life lived in relationship with God to water. But on a hot, blacktop road that scripture came alive to me. Under such conditions life is reduced to the basic essentials and one of the most basic is *water*. After walking miles in 100-degree heat it's hard to imagine anything could surpass the satisfaction offered by a glass of ice water. [And] Christ offers us living water with which we will thirst no more. Now I can truly appreciate the comparison.

Like the roads we traveled and any human experience, the Walk had its ups and downs. As Bishop Ben [a walker from Uganda] said one evening when referring to the pain in his feet, "There is no love without pain." We walkers grew because of our participation, many lives were encountered and touched along the way and over a million dollars were raised to provide shelter around the world.

Long-Lasting Effects

The consciousness-raising function of the Walk also raised money for Habitat, but it sometimes took a while for the dollars to come in. An exciting story will illustrate.

On the 1983 Walk (our first Walk—from Americus, Georgia, to Indianapolis, Indiana), near Chattanooga, Tennessee, our one advance man, Solomon Maendel, went ahead of us to the next little town up the road, Dunlap, to find us a place to spend the night. There were only about a dozen of us on the Walk at that time.

He went to the First Baptist Church and asked the pastor if the walkers could sleep in the church basement.

"Who is this group?" the pastor asked.

"Habitat for Humanity," Solomon told him.

"I have never heard of that organization. What do you do?"

Solomon explained that Habitat was a Christian ministry that built houses for low-income families. The pastor listened politely but he was not convinced to turn the church over to a bunch of strangers from an outfit he had never heard of. Finally, the pastor said we could stay in his back yard. "It's a warm night and I've got a hose pipe which you can use to take baths.

"Of course," he added, "you'll have to bathe with your clothes on because you'll be out in the open!"

Solomon accepted. The back yard would be our bedroom for the night.

The next morning was Sunday, so we asked the pastor if we could tell the people in the church about Habitat for Humanity.

"Our plans are already made for the service and there is just no place to squeeze anything else in. Sorry."

We decided to go anyway. In Sunday school Millard was able to say a few words about the work. Then, we all entered the sanctuary for worship. The pastor led the congregation through the order of worship and, finally, came to the last hymn. Everyone stood with their hymn books open, ready to sing. The pastor looked over at Millard. "Brother Fuller," he intoned, "you wanted to tell us about Habitat for Humanity. Well, I've decided to give you five minutes. Come up here and tell us your story but don't go over five minutes. You can see that everyone is standing with song books open. I'm not going to have them sit down because if I do you will probably go overtime!"

Millard got up and faced the church full of folks standing, waiting to go home. He knew he'd have to talk double time or lose them, and he also knew he'd be in trouble with the pastor if he went over five minutes. So he talked as fast as he could and crammed as much as he could of his usual thirty-minute speech into five. Then he invited people to sign up for our newsletter.

We heard nothing from anyone in Dunlap until December 1987, four and a half years later. Then, one day, out of the blue, Millard got a phone call.

"This is Charles Henry," the voice on the line said. "You don't know me, but I know you. You were in our church in the summer of 1983 when you and a small group of people were walking to Indianapolis. You spoke to the congregation with everyone standing with their song books open. I've never heard anyone speak so fast! But I haven't been able to forget what you said. My wife and I signed up to get your paper. We've been reading it and we believe in what you are doing. Since you were here, I have retired from my job. I was at home with my wife, enjoying retirement when along came a man who offered me a job. I didn't want a job. But he insisted. So, I took the job, and now I'm making money I don't need. That's why I'm calling you. My wife and I have decided to give all the income from my retirement job to you!"

Charles wanted to know where Habitat needed money. He said he had a special interest in our overseas work. Millard began to tell him about our work in various countries and when he got to Guatemala, Charles interrupted. "How much does it cost to build a house there?"

"About $1,500."

"O.K.," he said. "I'll put a check in the mail today. Use it to build houses in Guatemala." Two days later, we got his letter and check—$6,000, enough for *four* houses.

But that wasn't the end of Charles Henry's Habitat involvement, just as it isn't with many of our contributors. A few months later, Charles called us again. He had heard about the Jimmy Carter Work Project to be held in Atlanta in June 1988 and wanted to participate. Of course, we told him to come on.

Then one evening in Atlanta during that work project, Millard related Charles's story to all the builders. The next morning, Charles told with great enthusiasm about a man who came up to him after Millard's speech. The man said he had also retired and had gotten a new job. He said he was so inspired by what Charles did that he, too, wanted to give all the income from his job to Habitat! To be honest, we have no idea how many gave because of Charles Henry without ever telling us. We do know that Charles continues to work on his "retirement" job and send money to Habitat. Such seeds of inspiration planted on the Walks continue to produce in many ways and many places to our surprise and delight.

End of the Road

The Kansas City Celebration at the end of the 1986 Walk was unforgettable, too. When the walkers approached Kansas City, more people joined in and we all marched toward Barney Allis Plaza downtown. Someone did a rough count and said we were over 600 strong. Banners were up by scores—Northern Utah, the Ozarks, Tennessee, India, Zaire, and Nicaragua to name only a few.

Jimmy and Rosalynn Carter were waiting there to greet us, along with John Carlin, Governor of Kansas, Roy Blunt, Jr., Secretary of State of Missouri, John and Mary Pritchard, founders of Kansas City Habitat for Humanity, and hundreds of other supporters.

A group of bicyclists were also in the plaza. They had pedaled in from Eugene, Oregon. Led by Norman Shinabargar from Santa Rosa, California, this dedicated band had raised $50,000 toward our tenth anniversary goal.

The stirring speeches heard at that Celebration filled everyone with more enthusiasm than ever about the expanding work of Habitat for Humanity.

Andrew Young, Mayor of Atlanta and an international board member, said in his keynote address, "We are called to be a part of a kingdom not of this world, and to make this world reflect the kingdom. How do we do that? By being a part of the transformation that occurs when we give and receive out of love; by making bold economic statements, not only about the lack of profit from house payments, but about the abundance of spiritual profit gained by investing in Habitat for Humanity."

Rosalynn Carter reminded us that Jesus "identified with the poor—the poor in money, in spirit, in influence, in power. He not only identified, He also acted. And He let everyone know that this is just what He had come to do. Jesus has promised that we will do even greater works than He did."

Sumihiro Kuyama, Assistant Secretary to the General Deputy Administrator of the United Nations Habitat and Human Settlements Foundation, spoke to us about the size of the problem of homelessness and poverty housing. His sobering speech helped us to realize what a huge challenge lay ahead: a hundred million homeless people in the world and over a billion people living in grossly substandard conditions.

Tony Campolo, sociology professor at Eastern College in St. Davids, Pennsylvania, author, speaker par excellence, and member of Habitat's International Board, delivered one of the most powerful talks of the Celebration. While gesturing dramatically, he drove his points home to everyone: "We are not just about building houses—the government could do that! Habitat is building the kingdom of God. It is taking people who think they're nothing and helping them discover that they are something!"

Jimmy Carter, speaking in his characteristic low-key manner, delivered a powerful message, the essence of which was that he and Rosalynn were totally committed to the growing work of Habitat for Humanity. (Many of his remarks appear in Chapter 3.)

The concluding speech of the Celebration was given on Saturday morning by David Rowe, President of the International Board of Habitat for Humanity. His words were riveting and a worthy end to such a great experience:

"The miserable, disease-ridden, dispiriting, life-threatening hellholes in which one-quarter of the world is living are a scar upon the face of the earth, but worse, they are a challenge to the gospel and an insult to the Easter story. Such evil is a personal affront to us and we need to take it personally. I think that the success of our next ten years will be directly traceable to our ability to find, win, and put to work those people who sigh and groan, and teach them to shout and sing! We need people who will start out to walk, but won't mind stopping to stoop down. We need people who will stoop down, but then won't mind cleaning up. And we need people, who after cleaning up, won't mind straightening up again and keep moving. We need people who realize that spiritual ain't worth spit without sweat."

A Thousand Houses

That weekend during a press conference in Kansas City, Millard did something that sounded outrageous. He announced Habitat's intention to "build an entire city block in a week" in 1987 at a Jimmy Carter Work Project in Charlotte, North Carolina. And it was quickly decided that the project needed to be set within a larger context. So a goal was set to build a thousand houses in 1987.

The immediate reaction was shock. Fewer than 400 houses had been built in 1985 and approximately 500 were put up in 1986. To build a thousand houses in twelve months would mean doubling what had been done the previous year. Habitat for Humanity had never grown that fast before.

The challenge, though, was intriguing and had an appealing ring to it. A thousand houses in a year! That would be some fantastic accomplishment. The year 1987 had been designated "The International Year of Shelter for the Homeless" by the

United Nations. That was another strong reason to set the ambitious goal of building a thousand houses.

The various Habitat projects across the country and around the world were contacted and asked to set specific goals. As the responses came back over the next several weeks, everybody let us know they enthusiastically accepted the challenge.

A thousand houses in a single year—over *three houses on average must be finished every work day*. It was a stretch goal, but Habitat folks were committed. We felt positive it could be done.

An enormous boost to the thousand-house goal would be the Carter Work Project in Charlotte to be held July 27–31. Fourteen houses would be built there.

But that week inspired the really *big* idea: *Habitat House-Raising Week*. What was needed was a symbolic event that would express the incredible nature of this united front of activity—something that would convey all the wonderful things going on everywhere, not just the individual events. So the North Carolina blitz-building week was expanded to become House-Raising Week. While builders were building the houses in Charlotte, other Habitat projects all over the world would also be blitz-building during that same week.

The response was absolutely tremendous. Everybody geared up for it. Finally, the big day, July 27, arrived—the day described in the beginning of the book—and the blitzes started.

In Charlotte, 350 builders came from twenty-eight states and two Canadian provinces to join forces with Jimmy and Rosalynn Carter and several hundred local people to put up those fourteen new homes.

Bob Hope came to do a benefit which netted us over $30,000 and with the golf-club-shaped hammer Jimmy Carter handed him, he bent that nail as all of us looked on and cheered. And he wasn't the only well-known person hammering nails. Charlotte Mayor Harvey Gantt, U.S. Congressman Alex McMillan, country singer Tom T. Hall, Boston Mayor Raymond Flynn, and Enterprise Foundation President James Rouse all came to drive some nails and lend their support to the exciting event. The religious and business communities raised over a million and a half dollars in cash and pledges. Eighty-six churches were involved with both money and people. Banks, the real estate association, the media, the schools—everybody became involved to insure the success of the effort.

The local CBS affiliate, WBTV, conducted a one-day tele-thon at its own expense with a goal of raising $25,000—enough to build another house. When the campaign went off the air late in the afternoon, they had raised $33,000. The *Charlotte Observer* had daily feature articles about the blitz-building event, encouraging the city to get behind the effort.

On Friday afternoon, July 31, fourteen tired but incredibly happy families moved into completely finished houses. They had worked all week with the volunteers to build their own homes. That evening, thousands assembled in the Charlotte Coliseum to celebrate.

In the days ahead the results came in from other Habitat projects across the land and from abroad. It was awesome what had been accomplished. Over 200 Habitat projects had partici-pated, building, renovating, or helping repair over 300 houses—in just five days! Some of the houses were completed and the families moved in, as they did in Charlotte. In others, the finish-ing up work would be done in the weeks ahead.

In Boston, for instance, progress was made on putting up eleven units. Over 400 volunteers participated.

In Chattanooga, the Habitat project raised one house dur-ing the week and made great progress on two more.

Memphis volunteers worked on ten houses at three differ-ent sites.

The Habitat for Humanity affiliate in Garrett County (west-ern Maryland) built one new house and repaired or renovated eighteen more.

Pinellas Habitat for Humanity in St. Petersburg, Florida, and Kalamazoo Valley Habitat for Humanity in Michigan built one house.

In Michigan alone, groups in Detroit, Muskegon, Wexford County, Grand Rapids, and Lake County participated. The Lake County project put up two houses during the week.

Kansas City, Missouri, Habitat for Humanity raised one house, dedicated seven more, and broke ground for still another.

And in Trenton, New Jersey, the partner family for one totally rehabilitated house was presented their key while in Sacramento, California, the Acosta family had their new Habitat house dedicated and they moved in, amidst much joy and celebration.

Houses were also started in Dallas, Texas, Mount Angel, Oregon, and Muncie, Indiana. On Denver's southwest side volunteers made a good start on two four-bedroom, one-bath homes. Among the volunteers were several homeowners who had already received new Habitat houses. They wanted to "give back" to help people like themselves have a good house.

In St. Louis, a work camp of American Jewish Society for Service students teamed up with the local Habitat project to raise one house and do rehab work on a two-family home.

While blitz-building was going on all across our country, similar efforts were underway overseas. In Peru, people were building. In Lilongwe, Malawi, southern Africa, the blitz-building and dedication of two houses made national radio and television news.

Fifty volunteers built two houses in Alto Beni, Bolivia, and Zaire reported an unprecedented number of local volunteers during House-Raising Week, citing the inspiration of a former U.S. president who was also working and sweating to build houses for the poor during the same week.

And as leaders of Charlotte Habitat for Humanity were presenting Indian pastor David Purushothaman with a $35,000 check for the Habitat project in Khammam, India at the celebration on Friday night, Saturday morning was dawning in that south central Indian city and twenty homes, just built at a cost of a little over $1,000 each, were being dedicated.[5]

By anyone's standards, House-Raising Week was an almost unbelievable success. Hundreds of houses were built. Thousands of volunteers gave of themselves in a beautiful expression of God's love in action. And the hundreds and hundreds of news stories helped tremendously to make shelter a matter of conscience.

House-Raising Week was also a strong factor in pushing us over the top on our thousand-house goal. When final figures came in at the end of the year from all Habitat projects, we learned that we had exceeded our goal by more than 200 houses! Across the United States and Canada, the affiliated projects built or renovated over 400 houses, and overseas, 811 houses were built, 91 more than projected.

1988—A Gigantic Habitat Extravaganza: House-Raising Walk

Now, we were ready for some new challenges. The rate of growth was accelerating. Between 1985 and 1988, the number of Habitat project locations had doubled. Things were looking great.

Could 2,000 houses be built in 1988?

Why not?

Again, a rallying event was needed. This "happening," Habitat House-Raising Walk '88, would combine the Jimmy Carter Work Project concept, the House-Raising idea, a marathon walk, and Habitat celebration into one grand Habitat extravaganza! And it would pull together two elements: a symbolic consciousness-raising walk and an action-oriented house-raising effort.

The event would not only be a 1,200-mile walk, to celebrate our twelve years of Habitat, but it would also be a "traveling work camp." Walkers and builders would cover 1,200 miles over a period of twelve weeks, raise $1.2 million and, along the way, build or help renovate 120 houses. And the House-Raising Walk '88 would conclude in Atlanta on the weekend of September 15–17 with the Twelfth Anniversary Celebration.

House-Raising Walk '88 would begin in Portland, Maine on June 27. Builders would start the Walk in Portland with the walkers, but after the grand send-off, they would get into vehicles and drive south approximately a hundred miles and blitz-build for a week at a Habitat project. On Saturday, the walkers would arrive at the building site to dedicate the Habitat houses built that week. Over the weekend, both walkers and builders would participate in Habitat rallies, speak in churches, and spread the message of Habitat in every other way possible. This scenario would be repeated each week all the way down the eastern seaboard to Atlanta.

Elsewhere, affiliates in other parts of North America and sponsored projects overseas would select one or more weeks during the twelve weeks of the House-Raising Walk to have their own House-Raising Week blitz. Our overall goal for the summer was to build at least 400 houses.

Jimmy Carter would participate in three ways in the action-packed summer. During the week before the Walk, he and Rosalynn would help renovate five apartments in the North Central Philadelphia Habitat project. During the first week of the Walk, they would work on a huge blitz to build twenty houses in a week in Atlanta. Finally, President Carter would address the celebration in Atlanta at the end of the House-Raising Walk.

Building Excitement

Of course, the staff in Americus grew to handle all the ambitious plans. Greg Sandor, an outstanding young man who was on the advance crew for the 1986 Walk, was named head of the House-Raising Walk team. A whole wing of one of our office buildings became a buzz of activity as funds and "in-kind" gifts were solicited for the Walk, builders and walkers recruited, pledge packets sent out, news releases prepared and distributed, and plans laid in hundreds of towns and cities to receive the builders and walkers. The advance team had to get permission to march through scores of cities, arrange for police escorts on busy and dangerous highways, and line up churches and other groups along the way to feed and house hundreds of people for eighty days and host scores of rallies.

Blitz-building efforts were planned for thirty-three cities and towns on or near the Walk route. Recruited were 176 out-of-town builders from thirty-two states and twelve foreign countries to be joined along the way by an estimated 1,000 local builders.

The Walk team decided that the theme for the House-Raising Walk would be "The Excitement Is Building." That theme was surely appropriate to describe the feeling of everybody at headquarters in Americus and of the thousands of people who were going to be involved in the event in one way or another. A rough calculation showed us that 30,000 people would walk, build, host the walkers or builders for overnight sleeping, prepare meals, or, in some other way, be directly involved in the House-Raising Walk.

Tomorrow Tucker

Before we all set out to make it happen, Millard told the Habitat partners and co-workers in Americus a story. It was about a ten-year-old boy in Atlanta who would move into one of the twenty Habitat houses to be built there by the Jimmy Carter Work Project in a couple of weeks. His name is Tomorrow Tucker and in many ways he is like a parable of what Habitat for Humanity is all about. Habitat brings hope for tomorrow, not only to Tomorrow Tucker, but to hundreds and thousands of other boys and girls and their mamas and papas whose lives are affected in a positive way by Habitat for Humanity. All the events of the summer would be focused on lifting hopes and dreams and on dramatizing our cause in such a way that thousands of others would be inspired to join us.

Then everything was set into motion and Millard flew to Philadelphia to help the Jimmy Carter Work Project get up and running. Philadelphia was memorable for reasons beyond the great work of renovating those buildings. Although several hundred people worked on rehabilitating five apartments in the heart of the north central Philadelphia ghetto and the project was a success, the response was less than enthusiastic from many in the city.

In separate interviews, Jimmy Carter and Millard expressed disappointment in this lack of local support. The result was several news articles and a powerful cartoon which appeared in the *Philadelphia Daily News* (see next page).

There was also a moment in Philadelphia that Millard will never forget. One of the rallies that week was held at Bright Hope Baptist Church. A mezzo-soprano named Marietta Simpson sang "Bless This House" in the most incredible rendition of that song most of the crowd had ever heard. It was made even

Reprinted from the *Philadelphia Daily News*, Signe Wilkinson

more dramatic in the meaning it held because of what was being done in the North Central neighborhood.

Portland —On the Road

After the week in Philadelphia, it was time to start the walkers on their way from Portland, Maine. Millard flew there to meet Linda and over 200 walkers for the grand send-off, reminding them of the deep significance of their journey to Atlanta because in Clarence Jordan's Cotton Patch version of the Bible, Jerusalem was Atlanta. So, in a symbolic way, Millard pointed out that we were all on the way to the Cotton Patch "Jerusalem." We would sing our "theme" song, "We're Marching to Zion" (especially since Zion is another name for Jerusalem) often along the way and think of Clarence Jordan and his vision.

Atlanta — Building Like Wildfire

On Wednesday of that first week of the Walk, Millard flew to Atlanta. The scene was almost unbelievable. Twelve hundred builders already had all the walls up, trusses on, decking nailed down, and shingles on at least a third of the houses and more rapidly covering the remaining ones.

Jimmy and Rosalynn Carter had arrived at noon on Wednesday, just a couple of hours before Millard got there. They were already hard at work at house number six.

John Wieland, an Atlanta businessman and home builder, was building six of the twenty homes at the Carter Work Project with his own people as his contribution to the effort.

He caught our "volunteer virus" so severely that he soon formed a not-for-profit division in his company, John Wieland Homes, to continue helping Habitat for Humanity in Atlanta and to assist other nonprofit groups that were helping with the housing crisis. (In October 1989, John joined our International Board of Directors.)

Also, in an unprecedented move, Peachtree Presbyterian Church had given a $100,000 matching grant and its people had built the "test house" to near completion at the construction site to work out all the "bugs" in the building procedures and techniques. Scores of other churches had joined the city-wide effort to provide a huge chunk of the money and hundreds of volunteers needed for the project. (A year later Peachtree Presbyterian made a five-year commitment to raise and give $100,000 a year to Atlanta Habitat for Humanity and provide thousands of volunteers to help rebuild an entire neighborhood.)

Near the end of the project week at an evening rally, it was discovered that one house was behind schedule and would not get finished. So just as everyone was about to retire to dorm rooms for the night, Millard explained the situation and asked for volunteers to stay up and work so that all twenty houses would be finished on schedule the next day.

Of course, a host of people volunteered, including Jimmy Carter. The group worked until nearly 2:00 A.M. completing some vital sheet rock work. The next day, that house was finished right along with the rest.

Where only foundations were on Monday now stood twenty beautiful new homes, built by love in just five days and ready for occupancy. All painting done. Grass planted. Shrubbery and flowers in for every house.

Tears and Praise

At the heart-warming dedication, two homeowners, Evelyn Jackson and Marion Turner, were called forward to speak on behalf of all the families. With a mixture of happy tears and moving praise for the partnership and love they felt from all the volunteers who had come from throughout the United States and from Canada to build the houses, Evelyn and Marion thanked everybody for what they had done.[6]

And Bruce Gunter, leader of the Jimmy Carter Work Project, summed up almost everybody's feelings that day with words printed inside the front cover of the evening's program. They are thoughts that linger in our minds and hearts. He wrote:

> As gregarious beings, humans were created to live in community and to be mutually supportive and helpful to one another. In earlier times in this country, the "barn raising" epitomized that caring attitude. Revitalizing that spirit in this more cynical age, Habitat for Humanity has drawn, for twelve years now, on the highest motivations of people of good will and strong conviction to build and sell houses to people who would not otherwise be able to share in this counterpiece element of the American Dream. With no profit, no interest—terms at the heart of the Habitat formula—and leavened by volunteers, donated materials and money, and families willing to work hard to help themselves, Habitat regularly produces transformations in the lives of the participants.
>
> People whose lives were debased by the violence of poverty now pay taxes and become contributors themselves; suburban volunteers far removed from the pain of material deprivation gain more substance and sensitivity from a hard day's work for the benefit of

another. The rhetoric is backed by action, as Jesus admonished his followers to do. . . .

Twenty houses in five days! Twenty families! As we depart from here and go forth, carrying this message of joy and hope, we hold in our hearts the words of an ancient Hebrew writer, "Every house is built by someone, but God is the builder of all things."

Back to the Walk

Millard then rejoined Linda and the other walkers near Boston. By the following Sunday, we had walked to New London, Connecticut. There, about fifty of us boarded a ferry boat to Long Island, New York. We went directly to First Baptist Church of Riverhead (a predominantly black congregation) where a breakfast was in progress. We can still see the lively processional of the choir to the front of the sanctuary. From minute one, the service was an experience, to say the least.

When Millard stood to speak, he told the congregation that after he saw that processional he thought they should rename their church either the First Inspired Baptist Church or the First Fired-up Baptist Church. But when they served wine instead of grape juice, he was certain of it. They roared with laughter.

Then Millard told a story about a man who wanted to set up a wine-making company in a small northern Georgia town. The town council was made up entirely of teetotaling Baptists. They said they didn't want any wine-making business in their town. The wine-maker tried to win them over by telling them that Jesus' first miracle was turning water to wine.

"Yes," one council member said, "but that wine was different. It didn't have no alcohol in it and what you want to make does have alcohol in it!"

But then another member spoke up, "Well, brother, I don't know about that," he said to the first member. "I think the wine Jesus made had alcohol in it. Wine, by definition, has alcohol in it. Just to be honest, I really don't know why Jesus did that miracle. It's been an embarrassment to me all my life!"

The people exploded with laughter.

Millard went on to tell them that many of Jesus' teachings

are embarrassing—like "invite strangers in," "give your money away," "love your enemies," and "go the second mile." But, we Christians are called to obey even those tough teachings if we would be the salt, leaven, and light Jesus wants us to be in the world. And those tough teachings were the ones we wanted to uphold with our Habitat efforts.

Late in the day, we all reboarded the ferry boat and returned to Connecticut. The next day the Walk continued southward.

Since we were so near New York City, the two of us decided to catch a train in Westport and ride into the city to visit the construction site on the Lower East Side of Manhattan at 745 East 6th Street. The walkers would not be going to that site, but about twenty of the builders were there helping to renovate a six-story building for twenty-two families. The building across the street at 742 East 6th Street was already occupied by nineteen families, following renovation work done by Jimmy and Rosalynn Carter and several hundred other volunteers in 1984 and 1985. Everything still looked great.

Then Linda flew back to Georgia. Three weeks was about all the time she could allow away from duties at home and the office.

By week's end, Millard and the rest of the walkers had reached Philadelphia—a month after the work week there. A man dressed in a kilt and playing bagpipes led the walkers across the Ben Franklin Bridge and into the "City of Brotherly Love."

After a break at the Mall in downtown Philadelphia, the walkers, now expanded in number by a large group of Habitat people from the nearby York affiliate, headed toward the project in North Central Philadelphia where the Carters had worked on the five apartments. To get there the walkers had to pass through some of the worst slums in America, with garbage and graffiti and burned-out buildings everywhere.

But there is always a ray of light in such places. A simply dressed elderly lady stopped Millard and asked if the group took donations. When he responded positively, she pulled out a small bundle of money and extracted a ten-dollar bill. He asked for her name and address so he could send her a receipt. She gladly gave it to him. Then he invited her to come to the rally scheduled that evening. She asked where it was, so Millard reached in his back pocket for his itinerary sheet. As he was showing her the list, she pointed to his name on the sheet and exclaimed, "This man writes me letters!" When he told her he was that man, her face beamed. Here was a woman who had very little, but she generously shared to help others have a place to live. The bleak neighborhood did not look so bleak and hopeless with that woman standing in it.

Sleeping with the Homeless

Several days later, Millard and the other walkers arrived in Chester, Pennsylvania, where they were scheduled to spend the night in a shelter for the homeless. John Alexander, a member of the Walk team, led devotions that morning before the Walk started out. His sharing consisted of reading what he had written in his journal when he first visited Chester as part of the advance team. His entry told about a big woman named Hilda who was in charge of a shelter for the homeless in that city. Here was someone who gave totally of herself to serve the poor in her city. He told of how she once had backed a difficult man down with a baseball bat and how much sadness and sorrow she experienced when her son was stabbed to death on the front steps of the shelter. And with words that brought tears to many eyes, he then read, "Today I met Jesus. She was big and fat, with no teeth, and she was black."

A few days later, we arrived in Washington and then marched from the Capitol to the Lincoln Memorial. Atlanta Mayor Andrew Young was with us and made the major address at the rally. Linda had rejoined the Walk in Baltimore. Together, we trekked with the other walkers to Richmond, Virginia. In the weeks following, the walkers slowly made their way southward, passing through the Carolinas and into north Georgia. The builders raised up houses in Richmond and in Durham, Wake Forest, Orange County near Chapel Hill, Carrboro, Burlington,

Greensboro, Winston-Salem, Hickory, Statesville, Thomasville, Asheville, Davidson, and Charlotte, North Carolina; Greenville, Rock Hill, and Spartanburg, South Carolina; and Clarksville and Carrollton, Georgia. Finally, the House-Raising Walk arrived in Atlanta.

Hundreds walked by the Carter work site on Foote Street where Rosalynn Carter joined us. From there we proceeded on to the Carter Presidential Center. President Carter came out to greet us. Within the next few hours we had all finished the long walk, arriving at the Atlanta Civic Center exuberant and thankful. Twelve hundred miles had been covered, fourteen states traversed, 154 houses worked on or completed, and there had not been a single serious injury.

Time to Celebrate

Our Twelfth Anniversary Celebration was unforgettable; but the first evening was even more so because it was concluded by the original cast presenting excerpts of *The Cotton Patch Gospel*, the musical based on the Cotton Patch translations of the New Testament by Clarence Jordan. It was a fitting way to close a walk to Atlanta, the Cotton Patch Jerusalem.

When Millard spoke during the Celebration, he quoted a story from the great Broadway musical, *Man of LaMancha*, in which Don Quixote and his little servant Sancho were having an argument. As Millard told it, the argument grew louder and louder and angrier and angrier. Sancho kept insisting that the facts were the facts until finally Don Quixote screamed at him, "Facts are the enemy of truth!" Millard began to explain:

> We are always dealing with facts, but facts can often obscure the truth. We need to be people forever searching for truth. And you know, my Bible concordance has no reference to "fact" or "facts," but numerous references to "truth."
>
> The fact is that along the way on the House-Raising Walk, we've had blisters, been tired, sometimes depressed by the length of the road, and even

misunderstood on occasion. One man yelled from his car window as he passed, "Get a job!"

The truth is we've got a job—eliminating poverty housing and homelessness from the earth.

The fact is that three million people live in the streets and another twenty million live in poverty housing in the United States.

The truth is that we're committed to changing all that and reducing those figures to zero by making it socially, politically, and religiously unacceptable to have poverty housing and homelessness in the United States of America.

The fact is that worldwide a hundred million people are homeless; over a billion live in poor housing.

The truth is that the whole earth is the Lord's and the fullness thereof and we are equally committed to a world of zero homelessness and zero poverty housing.

The fact is that it will take billions of dollars to build houses for everybody.

The truth is that the Lord owns the cattle on a thousand hills and all the silver and gold in those hills and all the greenbacks in your pockets and purses, and God wants His cattle and silver and gold and greenbacks used for His purposes.

The fact is that our nation is armed to the teeth because we are afraid of our neighbors. Billions of dollars that could be spent on housing the poor are spent instead on bombs and guns. And not only is our nation heavily armed, but virtually all nations on earth are armed and busy trying to get more arms.

The truth is that through God's love we can beat swords into plowshares and spears into pruning hooks, we can transform nuclear devices into nails and helmets into hammers.

The fact is that we now have Habitat projects in nearly 400 towns and cities in twenty-eight nations, but there are hundreds of thousands of cities, towns, and villages throughout the world and most of them have some degree of poverty housing and homelessness.

The truth is that Habitat for Humanity is fast becoming a movement, spreading across the land and around the world into more and more places every day, every week.

The fact is that Habitat could never build enough houses for everybody.

The truth is we are becoming a conscience to the world, inspiring others to join us in this noble struggle. Everyone, working and building together, can accomplish the task.

The fact is that Habitat's approach of faith-inspired no profit, no interest, and sweat equity is naive and makes no sense. It can't work.

The truth is that the idea came from God. God's ways are not our ways, but they are right. When we try them, we are amazed at how the naive, nonsensical approach works.

The fact is that considering the immensity of the problem and the complexity of the situation, we cannot possibly hope to succeed in what we're trying to do.

But the truth is that, with God, all things are possible and, partners, we are marching ever onward, in lock step, with the Lord God Almighty.

Throughout the remaining months of 1988, building continued, with many houses worked on during the House-Raising Walk being completed and new ones started along the Walk route and all over the country and abroad.

But as hard as everyone tried, when the year ended the 2,000-house goal had not been met.

So in 1989 we all tried again—and succeeded. Actually, we went over 2,000.

Now, our sights are set on over 4,000 houses in 1990. And, by 1994—*10,000.* The excitement *is* building. There's no reason not to keep setting our vision higher and higher.

2

The Foundation — Jesus Christ

Habitat for Humanity is openly and unashamedly a Christian organization, as it follows Christ's teachings in providing shelter for needy families, inviting them into our hearts and lives. The idea was born out of the fervor of people who wanted to put their faith in Jesus Christ into practice.

We in Habitat try to put the love of Christ in every mortar joint, between every block laid and every board nailed.

But Habitat for Humanity is not a church. Instead, it is a servant of the church.

Our "theology of the hammer"[1] brings an incredible array of folks together—people who disagree on all sorts of things, both political and theological, but who can all agree on a hammer, the instrument of Jesus the carpenter. We all take our hammers and saws and levels and other instruments of the building trade and we work together, letting the world see that we Christians can agree on something! We can agree on a hammer and a nail, and we can and do drive nails together as a manifestation of God's love.

Millard tells audiences across the country that Habitat for Humanity does have one doctrinal point and that is if you don't have a Habitat bumper sticker on your car, you are living in sin. He says that in jest, of course, but like most jokes, there is some seriousness behind it since we do believe strongly in challenging everybody to join us in our worldwide effort to eliminate poverty housing and homelessness.

Everybody Welcome

Habitat for Humanity has an open-door policy—all who desire to be a part of this work are welcome, regardless of race, color, or creed. That's why one of Habitat's official purposes is "to enable an expanding number of persons from all walks of life to participate in this ministry."

Every House a Sermon

Do you know what we see when we work on a house? We see a sermon, and we want others to see the same thing. From the beginning, we have wanted to build and renovate houses which are sermons. What do we mean?

Jimmy Carter led a work project in Charlotte, North Carolina, in July 1987 to build fourteen houses in a week, the one you read about in the Prologue and again in Chapter 1. The 350 builders arrived from all over the United States and Canada on Sunday afternoon. By nine o'clock Monday morning, the walls were up on all fourteen houses. By noon, the roof trusses were in place and the decking was going on. Before quitting time, all the roofs had been covered with felt and all the doors and windows were installed. And the next morning, the *Charlotte Observer* ran, on page one, three full-color pictures of the work site—at 8:00 A.M., noon, and 5:00 P.M., showing the dramatic progress. The bold headline for that day exclaimed, "Christian Commitment Raises Roofs!"

The next morning, everyone was back at the site. Following devotions, we all fanned out to the fourteen houses and started putting the shingles on the roofs, nailing the siding on the exterior walls, and beginning the inside work. With all the support people running here and there, in addition to the hundreds of builders, the place was a literal beehive of activity.

Later that Tuesday morning, Millard was at one of the houses at the edge of the area looking over the sea of humanity before him and wiping sweat from his brow, when he noticed a man standing in the street a few yards away. He, too, was surveying the scene with a look of awe on his face.

"My goodness! Look at all the folks. I wonder who's paying all these people!" he said to no one in particular.

Millard walked over to the man and answered him. "No one is paying these people. They are all volunteers, working for nothing!"

"For nothin'? You mean they ain't gettin' paid nothin'?" he exclaimed.

"That's right," Millard responded. "They are all volunteers."

"Folks don't do things like that, especially in this kind of heat. Do these people know the families that will live in the houses?"

"No," Millard said, "they were all strangers before Sunday, But this whole situation is even worse than you think. These people are not only working to build these houses for people they don't know, as volunteers without pay, they paid their own way to come here to work for nothing!"

"Why would people do something like that?"

"Because they love Jesus. They believe this kind of thing is what God wants us to do for one another . . . to express love in tangible ways."

"Man," he sighed, "that's sho-nuff religion!"

He had seen the sermon, in fact fourteen of them.

And, of course, the people who move into Habitat houses know more than anyone else that they are sermons. Two years later, in September 1989, Millard was back in Charlotte preaching at Providence Baptist Church. After the first service, he asked one of the members to go with him to see the Habitat houses built during the Carter Work Project. His heart swelled with pride as he looked over the neighborhood houses, well-kept with the lawns neatly mowed.

As they turned around in the cul-de-sac and started driving slowly back up the street, they saw the house Jimmy and Rosalynn Carter had worked on. In the front yard a little boy, maybe six years old, was playing. They stopped the car momentarily, so the boy ran over to greet them.

"Hey," he said, "you got a pretty car."

"Yes, and you have a pretty house. Which one is yours?"

He waved a finger back toward the house.

"What's your name?" Millard asked him.

"D.J."

"Well, D.J., I want to ask you a question. Who built your house?"

Millard thought he would say, "Jimmy Carter." Instead, he quietly replied, "Jesus."

Jesus built his house. He knew. A mere lad, he had gotten the message. Habitat houses are sermons, and they preach for years, to those who live in them and to those who pass by.

When we lived and worked in Zaire in Central Africa, building the first overseas houses in this work, the local people referred to the housing project as, "Le Projet de Dieu" (The Project of God). The houses were called, "Les maisons de Dieu" (The houses of God).

For years, Millard has said in his speeches that every house built by Habitat is a house of God. We just let people live in them. He even tells homeowners they are sleeping on the first or second pew of God's house. Everyone laughs, but they get the message. This work is about putting God's love into action. Our work does speak for us and for everyone involved in this ministry. More importantly, it speaks for God.

Open Doors

Even though Habitat for Humanity is overtly Christian, we must be eternally open to and accepting of others, even those who have different motivations. We acknowledge, for instance, that Christians are not the only folks who know how to express love. Many non-Christians, especially Jews, are involved in various ways with Habitat for Humanity. We thank God for them and for their good help.

Late in the spring of 1988, Millard was in his office trying to cram several things, as usual, into a full day before calling it quits and going home. His secretary told him there was a lady on the line who insisted on talking to him. Millard didn't know her so he asked his secretary to find out what the lady wanted. She wouldn't say, stating again she had to talk to Millard. Reluctantly he agreed.

"Millard Fuller, you are a wonderful man!" the lady exulted when Millard said, "Hello."

Right away Millard knew he had made the right decision to accept that phone call.

"I'm glad you think I'm wonderful—but why?"

"I've just read your book, *No More Shacks!* and that's a wonderful book and you are a wonderful man!"

Millard was liking this conversation better by the minute.

"But," she continued, "there is one problem."

Millard thought it was all too good to be true. His mind raced, searching for the negative in the midst of such praise. Quick as a flash, he knew what it was. "You don't like the Jesus part of the book, do you?"

There was stunned silence on the other end of the phone. Then, "How did you know?"

"Well," Millard replied, "I've gotten other phone calls similar to this one. "I'll bet you live in New York."

"How did you know?"

"Well, I've lived in New York. I know a lot of people in New York and the way many of them think. I'll bet you've lived in New York all your life."

"That's incredible! How did you know?"

"Well, I just guessed."

For the next few minutes, they enjoyed talking to each other. She told him she was Jewish. When she said that, he exclaimed, "I've got good news for you. My wife and I were recently in Israel and we discovered over there that Jesus was a Jew."

"You didn't know that?" she fairly shouted.

"We also made another amazing discovery in Israel. All of Jesus' disciples were Jews."

"You didn't know that either?"

"Well," Millard confessed, "I did know that, but I was making the point that the Christian religion sprang from a bunch of Jews. We have a lot in common. The Bible tells us that God has a special love for the Jews. They're His chosen people."

She warmed up even more. She told Millard she and her husband had a small construction company just outside New York City and that she would like to see a Habitat project started there. Since the main purpose of Habitat for Humanity was to "proclaim the gospel of Jesus" she wasn't sure she could, in good conscience, serve on a Board of Directors, but she said she would get her Christian friends to form a board and she would help them raise the needed funds for building.

Millard then told her about the Jimmy Carter Work Project soon to be held in Atlanta in which twenty houses were going to be built in one week.

"That's amazing," she replied. "You're going to build twenty houses in one week?"

"That's right. Why don't you and your husband come down to help us do it?"

"But, I told you I'm Jewish."

"That's not the question. Can you drive a nail? Do you and your husband know how to build a house?"

"Yes," she replied slowly, "but there's another problem."

"What's that?"

She was silent for just a moment and then blurted out, "We're Republicans!"

"Oh, no!" Millard exclaimed, "God said He loved Jews, but He didn't say anything about Republicans. Come to think of it, He didn't mention Democrats either. I still think you should come."

She said she would talk to her husband and get back to us. In the meantime, she wanted to order some Habitat supplies including T-shirts for her family and would send a contribution immediately to the Habitat International office.

A few days later, we received a $1,000 gift from our new friend and a big order for more copies of *No More Shacks!*, the T-shirts, and other items from our store.

In the weeks following, she phoned Millard every day or two, always full of excitement about some new idea she had. A few weeks later Millard made a trip to New York to speak to a meeting of architects. She and her whole family met him at La Guardia airport. The first thing Millard saw was her children jumping up and down, dressed in their Habitat T-shirts, yelling, "There he is! There he is!" They drove him to the meeting and fed him lunch in their family van on the way.

They did decide to come to Atlanta. Her husband led a construction team that built one of the twenty houses. Afterward, she returned to her hometown and was very active in forming a local Habitat affiliate there. Later in the year, she visited us in Americus and went to Milwaukee with us for the 1989 Jimmy Carter Work Project there. We have come to love and respect this lady and her beautiful family. She is a special and appreciated partner in the growing work of Habitat for Humanity. She is not a Christian by her own admission. We know that God loves this lady and her family just as much as He loves our family. But, we are convinced Christians. We believe Jesus is who He said He was—the Savior of the world, that He is the way, the truth, and the life.

So, for us, we proclaim Christ. And yet, we always want to be open to those who don't, and Habitat wants to be open to those who don't, too. We know that Jesus and the cross are offensive to many, including some Jews and many other people who have not accepted Christ. The Bible tells us this, simply and plainly. Millard has been ridiculed and accused of being narrow and too sectarian. Some have written letters to our board members trying to remove him from leadership in Habitat for Humanity because he talks about Jesus so much. We mean no offense to anyone, but we both must proclaim what we have experienced and what we believe, and why we are doing what we are doing.

Across the country and abroad, though, we have non-Christians serving in Habitat projects. They are welcome and are considered partners in the work. They simply understand that they are working with an organization that has "sold out to Jesus"! And they believe what we are doing is still worth doing— which in itself is a powerful testimony.

For several summers, the fine organization American Jewish Society for Service in New York City has sent work groups to Amarillo, Texas, and St. Louis, Missouri, to work with the local Habitat groups. In their national magazine and in correspondence, they have expressed their appreciation for being able to work, as a Jewish group, with Habitat, a Christian organization. They have been warmly welcomed and appreciated. We hope this relationship continues and that other such relationships may evolve in the years ahead.

Nondiscriminating Selection

What does all this mean for the "partner families," the people who are selected for housing? From the beginning, we have always insisted on a nondiscriminatory family selection criterion for all Habitat projects, both in the United States and abroad. This simply means that neither race nor religion determines who receives Habitat houses. The only criterion is need. This philosophy and practice is consistent with the clear teaching of Jesus. God's love is universal. It knows no bounds. When Jesus fed the multitudes the only criterion for getting fed was being hungry. No questions were asked about whether the hungry folks believed Jesus or accepted His message. Food was simply shared with all because all were hungry.

But we do share the Christian faith with homeowners. A Bible is presented and a message delivered at every house dedication. The families accept the Bible gladly. And sometimes we receive something in return. During one house dedication service in Buffalo, New York, in late 1987, the partner family who happened to be Moslem returned our gesture by giving us a copy of the Koran. Both sides witnessed to what they believed. It was a joyous occasion.

Internationally, as you might imagine, this policy of need as the only criterion for housing is surprising to many. When we made our first trip to India in 1988 to visit Habitat's work in the state of Andra Pradesh, we participated in many house dedication services. Some were for Christian families, but others were for Hindus or Moslems. All received a Bible, but no requirements were made about conversion, church attendance, or anything like that.

Mr. Korabanda Azariah, president of that dynamic Habitat project in southern India, said a Hindu lady once went to local government authorities to ask if she must become a Christian to be accepted for a Habitat house. Mr. Azariah was called in by the official. His answer was correct and classic. "Tell the lady," Mr. Azariah said to the official, "that all she needs to know is that God loves her. There is nothing else. She was chosen on the basis of her need. That's all."

So, Habitat for Humanity has an open door for involvement. All church folks are beckoned to help, Protestant and Catholic alike—to drive nails, saw boards, and contribute financially. Also called are those who have a different motivation to do the same. And all in Habitat for Humanity are serious about serving God's people in need regardless of race or religion.

Scripture teaches that Christ breaks down walls that separate neighbor from neighbor. Through Him, we learn that God loves us all.

This firm foundation in Christ is so important that Habitat has resisted the ever-present temptation to accept government funds which carry with them the very great likelihood of changing that focus.[2] Habitat for Humanity wants to be a good partner with government; yet our roots, our motivation, and solid rock foundation in Jesus Christ must never be compromised to gain financial support from any source.

We began this ministry to put love for Christ and respect for His teachings into practice. Habitat houses are sermons—sermons of pure truth. People are attracted to truth in action. And that's what we always want to be.

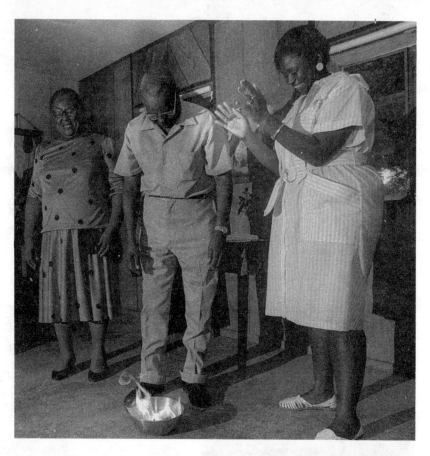

Betty Jean Jones of Koinonia, right, applauds after homeowners Bo and Emma Johnson drop the burning mortgage into a bowl.

In Puno, Peru, women enjoy putting up walls of their new home (Zenon C. Rojas photo).

Banner, designed and hand-crafted by Habitat volunteer Joan Burnett, carried and displayed on Walk route.

"Going once, going twice, SOLD for $350." Ted Swisher auctions off Millard Fuller's shoes at end of 1,000-mile Walk to Kansas City, Missouri (Steve Charles photo).

Walkers and bikers arrive in Kansas City for Tenth Anniversary Celebration.

Three House-Raising Walk '88 builders setting trusses for a new Habitat house in Richmond, Virginia (Lisa Verploegh photo).

Rosalynn Carter joins House-Raising Walk for "home stretch in Atlanta." Greg Sandor, Walk Director (right), enjoying triumph with John Alexander, Route Coordinator. Steve Baker, Coordinator of Habitat for Homeless Humanity, and David Austin carry Habitat banner.

Habitat Directors Andrew Young of Georgia and Frank Lennon of Massachusetts flank Millard Fuller as they walk down Pennsylvania Avenue in Washington, D.C. with other House-Raising Walk '88 walkers and builders.

Cheryl Fleetwood (left), Safety Coordinator, with Patty Dunn and Cindy Schultz on House-Raising Walk '88.

Florian Wanger of West Germany reaches out to congratulate Noah Kyireh of Ghana, West Africa — two of more than twenty international participants in House-Raising Walk '88 at the conclusion of the event in Atlanta.

3

Presidential Builders—Jimmy and Rosalynn Carter

Without a doubt, the single most significant factor in Habitat's explosive growth over the past few years has been the involvement of former President Jimmy Carter and his wife Rosalynn.

It began in 1984 when Jimmy Carter led a work group to New York City to help renovate a six-story building for nineteen families in the New York City Habitat for Humanity project. The Carters continued their active involvement after that. President Carter joined Habitat's International Board of Directors, and Rosalynn became a member of the Board of Advisors.

But as good as the former president is with a hammer and as adept as he and Rosalynn both are in attracting media exposure, he's also helped shape Habitat with his vision of what we could be.

In 1984, during a Habitat board meeting in Amarillo, Texas, Millard proposed a two-year $10 million fund-raising goal in connection with a Tenth Anniversary Celebration planned for Kansas City, Missouri, in September 1986. The year before, a $1 million goal had been easily met.[1]

Millard's idea was to achieve the ambitious new goal through gifts from corporations and foundations as well as from individuals and churches—-and from another marathon walk. Even though Millard detailed his reasons for believing

41

the $10 million goal was achievable, there was considerable opposition within the board to adopting it.

"It's not wise to go from a $1 million goal to a $10 million goal," one member exclaimed.

The arguments went back and forth.

Then Jimmy Carter spoke. He had been holding back on expressing his views since this was his first board meeting. But he had definite ideas on this fund-raising goal: "We should go for it. A larger goal will result in more money raised even if the total goal is not achieved. If we set a goal of $5 million, we may raise $3 million or $4 million, but if we set the goal at $10 million, we might raise the entire amount."

The board decided to go for the $10 million and Jimmy backed up his words with action. He agreed to chair a $10 Million Campaign Committee which was quickly formed and began brainstorming ideas to reach that "impossible"-sounding figure. Rosalynn volunteered to raise $10,000 personally and challenged people on our mailing list to do likewise, either raising $10,000 or as much as possible. This single idea produced over $130,000. President Carter donated thousands of dollars from honoraria given to him for speeches and he wrote personal letters to several wealthy individuals asking for contributions. He also sent out a mass mailing asking for support from new people. That effort produced 40,000 new donors and raised over a million dollars. Mayor Andrew Young, a member of the committee, wrote letters. One committee member got his company to give $45,000. Other companies donated hundreds of thousands of dollars worth of building materials and supplies. Various committee members personally gave over a million dollars. When the campaign ended in December 1986, the results of our combined efforts were totaled. We had raised not $10 million, but $12 million!

The Jimmy Carter Work Projects

But that wasn't enough "action" for the Carters. Probably one of the most critical factors in our astounding growth and success has been the highly publicized Jimmy Carter Work Projects. The 1986 Jimmy Carter Project was the largest one to that date. We'd attempt to completely build, from foundation up, four town-houses in five days in Chicago's West Garfield neighborhood as a part of the work of Westside Habitat for Humanity. For that time in Habitat history, it was an awesome goal.

As with most Habitat projects, plans for the work in Chicago were made with a lot of faith and little money. But both money and building supplies were ready when the crews, along with Jimmy and Rosalynn Carter, began work on Monday morning, July 8.

The largest number of volunteers ever at a Carter Work Project showed up. Among them was Chuck Colson, of Watergate fame and founder of Prison Fellowship. And he'd brought six inmates who had been given permission to leave prison to build with the Carters that week. A special local person was Tom Nayder, president of the Building Trades Council of Chicago. He made sure that union and apprentice laborers were there as needed—carpenters, drywallers, plumbers, electricians, roofers, landscapers—crucial help in Chicago.

Jessica Wallace, one of the happy homesteaders of the New York City Habitat project who had worked with President Carter the year before, came to work in Chicago. When he spied Jessica at the work site on Monday morning, he gave her a big hug. A *Chicago Tribune* photographer snapped their picture and it appeared on the front page of the paper the next day.

The homeowners-to-be were on the site, too. Arbie Nelson was one of them. She was living in a nearby condemned apartment with her family of nine. Electricity and water had been shut off. The week we were there a nest of rats fell from the ceiling onto one of the beds of her children. Buckets were used to bring water from a neighbor's house and the kitchen was a grill in the backyard. For this deplorable dump, Arbie paid $400 a month.

As the workers pounded the studs for the walls into place early on Monday morning, and as scores of people scurried around, taking measurements and yelling instructions, Arbie was overcome with emotion. She started at one side of the concrete slab and walked the length of it, with arms upraised, tears flowing from her eyes, crying out again and again, "It's a miracle! It's a miracle! Praise God. We're gonna have a house. It's a miracle!"

The Carters, of course, were the focus of most of the media attention. A slew of reporters made the work project front-page, prime-time news. Habitat for Humanity got "on the map" in Chicago and the whole Midwest during that week.

Even though the Carters were experiencing jet lag after a twenty-two-hour flight from Zimbabwe in Southern Africa, they worked the same long hours as everybody else. President Carter constantly challenged everyone to keep going. They didn't even take time off to celebrate their fortieth wedding anniversary. In fact, the Carters spent their anniversary and the entire week with the other workers in a run-down, three-dollar-a-day room in the nearby Guyon Hotel. They had linoleum on the floor and an orange crate for an end table.

It rained a lot during the week. That slowed down the work, but never stopped the progress. At several points, Jimmy Carter and all the other workers were soaked to the skin. Everybody just kept right on going. When someone commented one day that it was too bad that President Carter was soaking wet, Millard said they shouldn't worry because he's a Baptist and not afraid of water.

By Friday, all of the units were up, dried in, and just about finished. Units two, three, and four would need a bit more finishing work on the inside after we left. But Unit one was going to be finished. The new homeowners would spend that very night there.

The media had been alerted to the fact that the new homeowners would move in at five o'clock. This was an historic first at a Carter Work Project. A house, started on Monday, would be occupied on Friday. A veritable barrage of reporters set up their cameras on a hastily built platform at the edge of the yard. As the magic hour approached, machines were outside rolling out the grass while workmen planted shrubs and flowers. Inside, the last plumbing fixtures and carpet were being installed. Walls were being painted at the same time. And finishing touches were being done on the kitchen cabinets. Amidst this flurry of activity, Linda was hanging curtains in all the windows. A group of people had gone to the family's old house and loaded up the furniture. They now stood single file at the edge of the yard, furniture in hand, awaiting the signal from inside to bring it in. Then, at the dramatic moment of five o'clock, Linda emerged from the front door with the excited announcement, "It's ready!"

In went the family and their helpers, along with furniture. A tremendous cheer went up from all the workers and the scores of onlookers. Even the media people started yelling. It was high drama.

Later that month, we and the Carters were back in Americus to begin the thousand-mile Walk to Kansas City. Thousands of dollars had already been pledged for this marathon effort. A group of friends and admirers of the Carters had pledged $25,000 for their nine-mile portion of the Walk. And every year since, they have been a part of our bigger and better plans, always ready to help, always ready with ideas.

Former President Building Houses

The Carters' impact on publicity cannot be overstated. Over the years, their involvement has brought us exposure in such diverse places as editorial cartoons, national magazines, and television sit-coms. The media love what Jimmy Carter is doing. A former president is spending his time, not in luxury in some heavily guarded and plush enclave, not at fancy hotels and jet-set parties, but building houses for and with the people who need them. And the media have never ceased to tell Habitat's story when President Carter is involved.

But beyond media, the Carters' presence alone makes things happen when they need to happen. For instance, a boost was needed in the fund-raising efforts for the Chicago project, so ardent Habitat supporter Kris Ronnow, director of Community Affairs for the Harris Bank of Chicago, suggested that the bank host a fund-raising luncheon to which would be invited community, church, and business leaders. Thus one day, Jimmy and Rosalynn Carter, along with several others of us from Habitat, left the construction site in time to get cleaned up a bit. Then we headed off downtown. A list of "who's who" in Chicago was there to have lunch with President Carter. His presence made the difference. And that would be the story across the nation over and over in the years ahead.

Why Do They Do It?

Together, the Carters continue to be a tremendous influence and blessing to the growing work of Habitat for Humanity. And yet, they often go out of their way to express how much Habitat means to them.

In his keynote address in Atlanta at the Twelfth Anniversary Celebration, President Carter explained how he felt:

> Rosalynn and I have been working with Habitat now for a number of years. . . . We often get asked, "Why do you work with Habitat? What do you get out of it?" . . . As some of you may know, I was President of the United States for four years. But I get a lot more recognition for building houses in partnership with poor people in need than I ever got for the Camp David Accord or for SALT II or for all our projects in Africa and Asia or anything I do now since I left the White House. I can walk down the aisles of airplanes [talking to people] and invariably the number one thing that anybody ever says is, "Tell me about Habitat . . . ."
>
> Habitat is not a sacrifice that we make for others. Habitat is a blessing for those of us who volunteer to help others. It gives me a life of excitement and pleasure and adventure and unpredictability, to put it mildly. . . .
>
> You don't have to be a famous person, you don't have to be accomplished to participate in Habitat for Humanity as a full partner and with a great deal of excitement. Last summer there were 1,200 people who came together as volunteers in the so-called Jimmy Carter Work Project in Atlanta. Monday morning we had twenty empty concrete slabs. Friday noon, we had twenty completed, landscaped homes. And the point I want to make is that only two of us had ever

lived in the White House—1,198 people, just like you, just like I was, just like I am now. So, that can't be an obstacle in your mind about being an enthusiastic and permanent and lifetime and committed supporter of Habitat because you think it's not a worthy cause or because you don't think you have time, or you don't have the ability.

The Carters' way of building excitement for Habitat is contagious. People in projects around the world know how a former American president and first lady are joining the struggle for decent housing and they respond. The Carters' impact continues to invigorate us as we grow.

4

Dreams Coming True

Dear Habitat Committee,
    We have always lived in the same house. It is old, very small, and poorly built. There are no closets and, up until ten years ago, no bathroom and no running water in the kitchen. My father managed to borrow enough money to put a tub, commode, and sink on the cement back porch. It is very cold in the winter where you try to take a shower. We have a small gas heater in there but a lot of times the wind blows in through the cracks.
    Would you please help my family? I am a Christian and am trusting in the Lord to meet our needs. I know that He works through people to do His work. I have prayed about writing this letter and am sincere about what I have written you.
    May God richly bless you for what you have done for others.

Dear Habitat Committee,
    If it is at all possible could you please look over my application? I am a single parent with three children and we are living in a home with another all-adult family. I am renting only two rooms of this house. I pay a total of $100 a month, $50 for rent and $50 for utilities. The house is in very bad condition, there is only one bathroom which doesn't work proper and is not in the best shape, neither is the kitchen. . . . Parts of the house are falling in and are not safe for my children. We really need a place of our own. I would be able to pay for the house with the income that I have now. Please help us as quick as you can. I sleep in a bed with my baby boy, and my other boy who is four and my little girl who is six years old have to share a bed

together. I don't have a phone and neither does the family I'm living with but you can call me at the neighbor's house. . . .

These are typical letters received by Habitat for Humanity projects from people with a dream—a decent place to live that will give them a better chance at life.

Over the years, Habitat for Humanity has seen many people moving into decent housing, usually for the first time in their entire lives. What a joy it is to see dreams coming true and prayers answered.

Habitat homeowners are very special people. Let us introduce you to some of them, so you can hear their stories, see their struggles, courage, and determination, and take delight in their expressions of thanksgiving.

A Decent House

In Orlando, Florida, Willie and Virginia Franklin moved from a terrible shack. Virginia had been injured when she fell through the rotten kitchen floor. Now they are happily settled in their lovely new home. It is located in the Callahan Neighborhood which previously had a bad reputation. Now occupied by a number of Habitat families, the area no longer has trash and garbage strewn around. Willie has taken it upon himself to help clear the area of drug pushers. As he says, "I'm doing this for my children." Willie's sweat equity requirements completed, he helps out by serving on the Family Selection Committee of Greater Orlando Habitat for Humanity and works at the construction site on Saturdays. Often he wears his green "Kiss Me, I'm Irish" T-shirt which gains him the title of "Mr. Orlando Personality of the Year" from his Habitat co-workers.

Cassandra and Ivan Harvey of Kansas City, Kansas, have four children. A few years ago, life seemed to be falling apart. Ivan had a good job working as a painter and drywaller. Then one of their daughters became very ill. Since they had no insurance, her care took all their savings. They were forced to move from their rented home into a building owned by Cassandra's sister which used to be a bar and now was just one big room.

Without bedrooms or bathroom facilities, they lived there for three and a half years. To take a shower or use the toilet, they had to walk a block to the sister's house. Then about this time, to make matters worse, they learned that Social Services was suing them for $25,000 worth of medical bills. Ivan began drinking because of all the stress.

The Harveys applied and were accepted as Habitat partners. As soon as they found out they had been selected to receive a home, they both started working to get in their sweat equity hours. While their home was under construction, Ivan slept at the site to help prevent break-ins. The daughter's health improved and their lives started turning around. With the help of Habitat friends, the Harveys did not go to court and the amount of the suit was reduced to $2,500. Also, they have gone back to church. Ivan has been ordained as a deacon.

Virginia Hubbard of Lynchburg, Virginia, has been a Headstart teacher for more than twenty years. This is a very low-paying job lasting only nine months per year. She is a single parent with two sons, Jeff and Tim. The family lived in a basement apartment for fifteen years before becoming Habitat partners. "The salary I was earning made it impossible to get ahead. Every time I would get a raise, the rent would go up," she told us.

When she was selected to be a Habitat homeowner, Virginia spent a large part of her time helping people in the area understand Habitat. That was not difficult because she had taught most of the children in the neighborhood where the Habitat houses were being built. She said, "I felt welcome right away. Everybody was helping as my house went up. They brought in food and water, and allowed the builders to use their phones and refrigerators." Because the construction work was done around the clock in a blitz-building effort, the neighbors had to put up with a lot of extra noise but they didn't mind. Watching her house go up, Virginia exclaimed, "I just can't believe it, but I've got to because I'm standing here looking at it. This house was built for me by God's people."

She and her boys moved in the night the house was ready. For her sweat equity, Virginia did speaking and office work for the affiliate and worked on a Habitat home down the street from her house by helping to do drywall. On a recent speaking assignment she said, "I will volunteer myself whenever needed. I want to challenge and encourage all of you to express your faith in action."

Mr. and Mrs. Francisco De La Sancha of Deland, Florida, have eight children and work in a fernery. At the time Habitat met them they lived in a one-room travel trailer within a few feet of the drainage area for the fernery. They only had one bed, so the children slept on the floor. Yet the children always were clean and very polite.

Habitat learned of them when their four-year-old son drowned in the drainage ditch. Teachers visiting the family after the child's death were appalled at the family's living conditions and called the Habitat affiliate to see if something could be done.

The De La Sanchas were selected for the very first Habitat home built by West Volusia Habitat for Humanity. The family put in 501 hours of sweat equity. Among other tasks, they poured oil on the footers, painted, cleaned, and Mr. De La Sancha helped pour the concrete floor.

When the son drowned, Marisol, the oldest daughter, a straight-A high school student, became very depressed. Soon she was not doing well in school. As a result of the love the family received through their Habitat friends, Marisol's teachers said she recovered her former happy disposition. In fact, the whole family is very happy. Marisol translated her parents' description of how they felt about their new home: "We had never hoped that something as good as this would ever happen to us, not even in our dreams!"

In My Day

Roger Cross, of New York's Flower City Habitat project in Rochester, was having an interview with a prospective partner family. The grandfather, visiting from Texas, suddenly exclaimed, "I wish there was a Habitat in my day. I used to come home at night after working two jobs and I would find my family no better off than when I left them that morning. It was very depressing. We just couldn't get ahead, and the places we had to live were terrible. One day I realized that my family would be better off if they were on welfare. I don't like that idea, but it was better than what we had. And the only way my family could go on welfare was if I left them.

"I loved my wife very much. I loved my children very much, but the only way I could give them a better life was to leave them, so I did."

As tears rose in that grandfather's eyes, he added, "Oh, how I wish there had been a Habitat program for my family."

In Oklahoma City, Joe Bell, an elderly gentleman, was the recipient of the first Habitat house. Living with his daughter, he slept on a lumpy couch in the living room. This couch did not convert into a bed; he just crumpled up on it at night. The only place he had to put his meager belongings was behind the couch.

The day of Joe's house dedication, he cried when he was presented with a Bible. He said, "I have never had a home of my own before. I feel just like a king."

Since then two other Habitat houses have been renovated in Joe's neighborhood. It has taken on a completely new look. Where there were weeds in the yards, trash scattered around, screens torn half off, and junk cars parked, there are now neatly mowed lawns, trimmed hedges and no junk in sight. Home-owners and renters alike have fixed tattered screens and broken steps. They have mended porches and painted houses. And Joe Bell is everywhere, being a good neighbor.

Take Others First

Verniece Henry, also of Oklahoma City, is a young divorced African-American mother of five sons, four of whom are still at home. She had been living in a house with someone under very stressful conditions but later rented a small two-bedroom apartment of her own.

Members of the Family Selection Committee were a little surprised when they saw how nice Verniece's apartment looked. However, they soon found that the furniture had been picked up at the dump or at garage sales. (Verniece can take a yard of cloth and some varnish and make a piece of junk look like an antique.)

Verniece and her sons have worked on Habitat houses for others until they have accumulated more than 100 hours of sweat equity. But she keeps saying about every family who applies for a house, "They live in worse conditions than I do, so let them have the next house. Even though our conditions are very crowded, they are not intolerable."

The last three houses have been for white families; but Verniece has not looked at the color of their skin, just at their circumstances. Verniece and her boys will get the next house.

What has impressed the committee most about Verniece has been her sweet spirit of concern for others. She said, "I just know the Lord will supply our needs when we help others."

Changed Lives

"It would take an act of God to make this house livable!" These words were spoken by a neighbor before renovation began on Allen and Susan Dool's house. Vacant and boarded up for several months before being purchased by Central Oklahoma Habitat for Humanity, it did look pretty hopeless.

Working primarily on Wednesday evenings and all day Saturdays, Habitat volunteers completely renovated the house between December 1987 and April 1988.

Susan, along with her ten-year-old son, Shawn, worked alongside Habitat volunteers on this part of the project as well as other phases of the rehabilitation.

But the story doesn't end here.

Soon after the Dool family moved into their newly remodeled Habitat house, the mother expressed concern for Shawn. She confided that he had been stuck in third grade at school for three years and did not seem to be improving. The future looked bleak and discouraging for the boy.

One of the Habitat board members located a tutor who volunteered to give Shawn two private lessons weekly for whatever length of time would be required to enable him to learn how to accommodate his learning disability. A volunteer car pool was arranged for the tutoring sessions. Another board member agreed to chauffeur Shawn to a weekly after-school program which the tutor suggested would be beneficial and enriching for him.

Shawn's life has been redirected in wonderful ways, all beginning with his house being redone. He entered fourth grade the next fall.

Alberta Patterson is Habitat's sixth homeowner in Waco, Texas. She is a mother of seven with five still at home. The youngest has Down's Syndrome. Alberta can see the change her Habitat house has made in her children: "I don't want this to sound wrong, but I feel that a lot of people take love for granted. Those who haven't had it in a family unit are starving for that love. Of course, I knew God's love; I had experienced that. But there is a need for natural love, and there's an emptiness in you until you find it. . . . That's what Habitat is all about. People have got to care to be a part of Habitat, because there's nothing else in it for them. Their happiness came from my happiness. To me that's what love is. The love is something I'll never forget. It has changed my life. And it has changed my children's lives.

"I would take the children to the new house, and tell them about the different groups of people who had come and worked on their home, and they felt like these people really cared about them. Because of the things we had been going through, they had begun to feel that there wasn't very much love left. But now they see these people who are doing something for them, who really seemed to care."

When No Others Can

Often Habitat can help when no others can. The Han family had been in America for four years, but life was still harsh. Life had been good in Vietnam. Mrs. Han was an eminent surgeon in Hanoi and Mr. Han was a noted writer. For three generations this Chinese family had lived in Vietnam.

With the communist takeover, life became difficult. As persecution against the Chinese minority increased, the Han family fled to Saigon. When South Vietnam fell to the communists in 1975, the persecution moved south, too. After spending some time with relatives in China, the Han family made a clean break with their past and immigrated to the United States. In a little more than a decade the family had lost everything—home, jobs, prestige, extended family. They faced life in an utterly foreign culture with no language skills and no opportunity to continue their professions. And they had five school-aged children.

When Habitat for Humanity of McLean County, Illinois, first learned about the Han family, they were living in a tiny two-bedroom house with a leaky roof. Water ran down the kitchen and bathroom walls when it rained. Furniture was pushed to the center of the already crowded room; buckets caught the drops that came through the ceiling.

Mrs. Han worked in a laboratory, a job which gave her little opportunity to improve her English. Mr. Han had two minimum-wage jobs. The two older daughters were at the local university—both had full class loads and carried two jobs. Neither lived at home because seven people simply could not fit in their house. Two other daughters were in high school; the son was in junior high.

Connie, the nineteen-year-old daughter, told what happened:

"One day last fall (1985), after an especially bad storm, I knew my family could live [in that house] no longer so I called the Financial Aid Office at the university where I am a student. But that office told me they could not help my family—they only help students. The lady suggested I call City Hall. They gave me more phone numbers and I called them all. But I found no help for my family, so I called the Financial Aid Office again. This time the lady referred me to Alan Martin, a contractor, who suggested my family apply for a Habitat house. He even got me an application.

"I applied and I waited, with big doubts that my family would be chosen to buy a house. Then one night . . . I returned to my room at Home Sweet Home Mission [one of Connie's two jobs was at the mission, where she was a live-in staff person], exhausted from a night exam. Waiting for me at the front desk was a mountain of messages, all from Mary Ann Johnson, the chairperson of Habitat's Family Selection Committee. Because the word 'urgent' was written on the message, I dared to call her so late. *'Good news!* Your family has been selected to receive a home!' she told me. My exhausted brain came to life."

In February 1987, the family moved into a four-bedroom Habitat house within walking distance of the university, the high school, and the junior high. Happily, all seven are under one roof, one that does not leak. Life is still not easy, but the family's basic need for simple, decent shelter has been met.

Even before moving into their home, Mrs. Han planted three rose bushes on the south side of the house. As the yellow roses waved in the summer breeze, they heralded a new beginning. They told the world that despite the darkness of winter, life does burst forth anew, and that for this family new life had come from death and destruction.

Not Even a Shack

Sometimes the Habitat partner family has not even had a house at all. In early 1988, a homeless family of seven migrated to Fayetteville, North Carolina, seeking employment. They came with no money and were forced to live in their car in a rural campground. A local Methodist minister befriended the family and through his efforts, housing in a small mobile home and employment for the husband were found.

At the same time, a house in Fayetteville was destroyed by fire. The out-of-town owner called a local realtor to have the lot cleared and sold. Mrs. Dean Russell, wife of Fayetteville Habitat's chairman, persuaded the owner to donate the lot to Habitat, citing this family's needs. By "chance," the lot on which the house burned was but a few blocks from the church which had helped the family and only two blocks from the husband's work. The children did not have to change schools.

Beyond the Problems

Dreams don't come true without hard work and problems, of course. It's sometimes difficult for people from varied backgrounds to work together without friction. The miracle is that through faulty humans, with all our imperfections and own needs, all of us can still reach past ourselves to help others.

Habitat homeowner Margaret Delucenay in Elkhart, Indiana, learned this reality as she worked with others to build her home:

"God had . . . promised me a nice home in a good neighborhood, but I didn't know how He was going to pull that off with my little $15,000 per year income. We were too poor to get ahead, but we made too much money to get any help. I read in the local paper that Habitat was looking for a partner family and felt a perfect peace about the Habitat vision (partnership housing). After being accepted as our town's 'first family,' I was on a cloud for weeks.

"After a while, reality struck and I found out that these Habitat 'angels' were really just ordinary people. They didn't always understand me and I just couldn't always figure out what they didn't like about me. They would ask me my opinion and then get very upset when I gave it to them. I wanted to forget about being a partner family and just get in line at Christmas time. That's when God gave me the vision of the 'calling' of the partner family. It was then that I realized that rich people needed help in understanding the poor just as much as I needed to understand where they were coming from.

"In the five months that it took to complete the house, I learned a lot about my own inability to relate to these well-to-do folks. You see, I hadn't been sensitive to the people that were trying to help me. I hadn't considered that they too have their agendas and past hurts. They were each caring individuals trying to respond to God's call on them to be a friend to the poor in Elkhart, Indiana."

The Same Everywhere

International stories are especially interesting, because of the difference in cultures and the aching need. Habitat representative Alice Miller wrote from Basankusu, Zaire, about the impact a simple gesture had on her:

"There are lots of days I feel like I'm just working with a construction company only building houses. Then an older woman comes to my door to pay some on her house. I invite her in and she talks about how God has helped her to have this house. She and her husband were chosen but before the house got started, her husband died. Some of her older children came out, cleared the lot, dug the foundation, and did the other work needed. She moved into her house last month and is paying for it by selling things from her garden. Yes, God is at work here, both in other folks' lives and in mine."

Donna and David Minich, Habitat workers in Tumung, Papua New Guinea, wrote us about one of their Habitat partners:

"Mayu Malet was one of our first Habitat homeowners. He has a wife and four children. We remember watching him, sitting and staring over the site where his house was to be built— hoping and dreaming! He worked every day on the construction of his house. When he made his first house payment, he proudly handed Donna the money (in coins and small bills) and he had good reason to be proud. The payment was more than was required and it boosted our depleted monthly allotted project funds so that we could continue to buy materials for the next house we had started building. Mayu's house is kept clean and in good repair. He always has some home improvement project going, like building shelves. His wife not only keeps the inside swept clean, but she sweeps the ground around the outside of the house, too. In their living room hangs a picture of Jesus.

"Mayu said: 'I never thought I would sit down in this kind of house or have enough money to build one like it. It was only a dream and now I live in this house. . . . Between Papua New Guinea and the United States is the big, deep, blue South Pacific Ocean. The countries and people are different in customs and languages. Before now, we did not know each other. But in a hurry we've met and are partners.'"

Ray and Gloria Cunningham in Kasese, Uganda, tell of two of their partner families with pride:

"Mrs. Jane Kintu, a single mother with four children, rents a small cubicle in the market place where she sells matches, soap, batteries, cloth, and some homemade articles. But now few people buy, so she has had to close her shop several days a week. Chosen to receive a Habitat house, she is happy that she can spend extra hours at the site helping to build her house and her neighbor's house, but she wonders how she can now afford to make the bricks and pay the necessary down payment.

"She told us, 'One thing I know. God is greater than all my problems!'

"The Kamonde family worked with vigor and enthusiasm on their house, but now are unable to buy and transport more bricks. Their funds are locked up in a nearly bankrupt co-op. Ray suggested that the family use the earth shoveled from the freshly dug twenty-foot pit-latrine to make bricks right there. Saturday morning we saw the family's two teen-age sons using a wooden form making three bricks every two minutes.

"We are impressed by people like Mrs. Kintu, the Kamonde family, and the many volunteers who walk two to eight miles to work at the site."

Housing Makes a Difference

Changed lives. Dreams coming true. Prayers answered. People just needing a start. Over and over we hear the stories. In Mount Angel Habitat for Humanity in Oregon, Ivo Bauman often visited an Hispanic family with five children, while their house was being built. One night, Lucy, their fifteen-year-old daughter, was home alone. Grateful for someone to talk to, she poured out her story to Ivo: "At the end of my first year of high school, my father told me that I could not return to school because the family needed income to live." She was working in a horticultural nursery twelve hours a day, seven days a week. She was beat. Demoralized. There was no spark of hope. And one day something awful happened at work. Her hand was severely mangled by a machine. It took extensive surgery and several months of physical therapy to rehabilitate her hand back to usefulness.

But then her family moved into their Habitat house. And their reduced monthly payments made it possible for Lucy to continue her education. She is still working but only forty hours a week now. Hope and joy have returned to her life.

Gussie Butler of Pensacola, Florida, invalid and elderly, was sharing her tiny "shotgun" house with five grandchildren. The old shack leaked badly and was propped up with poles on one side to keep it from falling over. When the dedication for her new house was held, she lay in her bed praising God and Habitat for getting her out of the rain and away from the rats.

Also in Pensacola, J. B. and Trudie Johnson and their two children lived in a tiny garage, all of them sleeping in the same room. J. B. had begun a house before he was laid off from his job. He wanted a home so badly he salvaged big timbers from a school building being torn down, and cement blocks from an old service station which was being replaced. He had been working two jobs at minimum wage, delivering lumber and cleaning a store at night, but he could not ever get ahead enough to finish the house. Today—with Habitat helping—the family has a beautiful, comfortable home.

Penny Hyde is a young, attractive divorced mother of two children. Her house had no lock on the front door. She was securing it with a big bucket of dirt. Windows were broken out, and there was no running water because the pipes had frozen the previous winter.[1] Habitat repaired her house. Penny said, "Getting the house repaired renewed me. I became a new person!" She's recently completed training at Pensacola Junior College to become a registered nurse, earning her own way by waiting tables.

When Bessie Grays and her two children in Amarillo, Texas, moved into their new Habitat house, they unpacked their boxes of clothing and linens on the driveway before taking them inside—to make sure they didn't carry any bugs from their old home into their new one.

Ted Hagen of Kingsport, Tennessee, tells about Norman Gillenwater's changed life: "I was working with Norman on a brick walkway for his Habitat house. The weather was warm and we had escaped to the shade of an old apple tree when the following conversation occurred:

"Norman said: 'Ted, you know I can't read, don't you? My daddy took me out of school when I was in the third grade. Until we built our house I didn't know how to do any work except a little farming and roofing. I learn fast when someone teaches me hands on. Working on this house I learned how to pour footings, lay block, do framing, siding, sheetrock, painting, flooring, trim-work . . . I'm a bigger man now.'"

Ted said he responded: "Norman, you just gave me the biggest pay day I've ever had!"

Habitat Owners Give Back

And the Habitat owners do give back. Rosie Simmons of Chicago makes that clear in her letter to us:

"Through Habitat I now know how to put on a door knob. I can fix a hole in the wall. I am getting ready to return to school, and I am looking forward to starting a new job, one that will provide more security and allow me to spend more time at home with my children. My children can now see life from a different view.

"Habitat has given me hope. I won't stop here, I will continue to move forward and I will continue to love Habitat and work in any way I can. I thank God for Habitat, that 'giant eraser' that continues to erase the lines that separate black from white, rich from poor, educated from uneducated, and one denomination from another."

A Place to Study

For Phat and Lieng Do, their new Habitat home means something even more—enough space for each of their children to have an adequate place to study. The Dos, who came to the United States as political refugees from Vietnam like the Hans, just recently moved into an Amarillo (Texas) Habitat home. Phat had earned his bachelor's degree in public administration and was working as an administrator for the government of South Vietnam. "Then the communists took over my country in 1975 and put me in prison for six years," he explained. Life was hard in the re-education camp, but Phat eventually found his family.

"Starting over is not easy," said Phat, who worked as a dish-washer when he first arrived in the States. "We came with bare hands," added Lieng, a former elementary teacher in Vietnam.

Their children, all "A" students, seem to have caught their parents' spirit and determination. Nam, who was about fourteen when they arrived in Amarillo, said he spent all his time learning English the first three months so he would be able to use it well enough when school started. He's now an honors graduate and is a pre-med student at Amarillo College while working part-time at St. Anthony's Hospital as a food service aide. He and his brother, Duy, share their own bedroom and each has his own desk. Duy is a member of Young Astronauts of America.

"To have a house is to have a future, a stable life," said their father Phat.

Miles and Elma Richmond, former Habitat volunteers in Lilongwe, Malawi, shared with us a letter they received from a friend and Habitat homeowner which shows the great value Habitat families in Lilongwe place on their new homes:

Dear Mr. and Mrs. Richmond,

We hope that you on your part have this one consolation that you were associated in laying the groundwork of charitable effort so that the kingdom of God and every other human ideal can become reality. . . . You have developed an understanding heart of the problems of less fortunate people where others would say don't cast your pearls before swine.

In our view, your organization continues to do something better, wiser and more valuable than anything Ministers [government] and Presidents have done in your country.

Yours very sincerely,
Mr. and Mrs. Kamangeni

Down with Crimes; Up with Dreams

One of those presidents, Jimmy Carter, in a speech given at a Habitat celebration, explained what impact he believes decent housing has on families:

"Drugs, crime, education, health care, and dreams for the future don't seem to be directly related to housing, but you know they are. This past summer, Rosalynn and I led a group of workers in Philadelphia. . . . One of the most vivid things we learned [there] was taught to us by a woman who had moved into a Habitat house shortly before we arrived. She pointed out that she had children, including some teen-age boys, who were a constant source of concern to her. When night came, she never knew where they were. She knew they were running around in a crowd that was often in trouble—even being imprisoned on occasion. And she could see her children going to a life of crime, ridden by drugs. And then she got a Habitat house; and all of a sudden her boys started coming home and they brought their friends home with them. And they told their mamma, 'Before we got this house, we were ashamed to let any of our friends know where we lived.'

"I've talked to Habitat mammas and daddies who didn't finish high school themselves—who never thought about finishing high school. Their parents didn't finish high school. Then just a few days after moving into a Habitat house, sometimes even when they were moving in, they began to talk about which college their children were going to attend. So, does housing have anything to do with crime? With drugs? With education? With ambition? With dreams? With happiness? I think so."

There's No Place Like Home

A thank-you card was sent by the Bult family to South Brevard Habitat for Humanity in Melbourne, Florida. It read: "Home Sweet Home—A very special Thank You to Habitat for Humanity, and also to all the wonderful people who were involved in making our dream possible. . . . Without the loving and caring of friends our home would still be only a dream. It is very hard to describe our feelings, except to say, 'There Is No Place Like Home.' Thank you. Sincerely, Ron, Debbie, Michael, Jeremy, Shane, Logan, Hannah, and Twinkie."

At Christmas 1989, we received a beautiful letter from eleven-year-old Ryan Brown of Key Largo, Florida. Here's what he wrote: "Dear Millard and Linda Fuller, Hope you have a very Merry Christmas and a Happy New Year and I thank you for bringing Habitat down to the Keys because me, my mom and my brother and my cat got the first house in Key Largo."

You can imagine how letters like these warmed our hearts.

Indeed, Habitat for Humanity builds houses. But as is obvious from these stories, there is a lot more to what happens than house building. It's making a house a home, a neighborhood a safe and beautiful community, building "bridges" between people of other cultures and classes; it's learning new skills, finding new ways to serve, acquiring new friends, and much, much more.

It is dreams coming true for all involved—dreams that translate into making a stronger society, a better world.

Ten-Million-Dollar Campaign Committee pose with Committee chairman, Jimmy Carter. Left to right: Linda Fuller, Ron Yates, Millard Fuller, Vada Stanley, George Anderson, Glegg Watson, Jimmy Carter, Ted Stanley, Landrum Bolling, John Pritchard, Deen Day Smith, Keith Paul, Andrew Young, Keith Jaspers, David Rowe (Wallace Braud photo).

The test house built by Peachtree Presbyterian Church volunteers in preparation for the Carter Work Project in Atlanta, 1988 (Ray Scioscia photo).

Former President Carter's work apron shows signs of heavy duty work.

An awesome pair, Jimmy and Rosalynn Carter install lapboard siding in Milwaukee (Ray Scioscia photo).

Linda Fuller packs insulation around window in Milwaukee (1989).

Millard Fuller and Jimmy Carter install kitchen cabinets during Carter Work Project — 1989 (Ray Scioscia photo).

Rosalynn Carter works with Habitat homeowner Cecila Dukuly (Bob Lucas photo).

Hazel Carter (Americus,
Georgia) in the yard of her
new Habitat home.

Lindsey Edge (right) presents Bible
to new homeowner Mae Vester
Coleman at house dedication in Americus.
Carol Pezzelli Wise, Karen Higgs and
Hattie Pitts with children in the background
(Ray Scioscia photo).

Single parent, Bob Stone, is first homeowner at Seattle Habitat. Bob is an active member of the Family Selection Committee and volunteers as project director on house renovations (Seattle Habitat for Humanity photo).

Kathe Gibson, left foreground, presents a welcome mat to the Dool family during dedication of their house on May 1, 1988, in Oklahoma City. The Dools — Allen, Susan and son Shawn — are all decked out in Habitat T-shirts.

5

Infectious Habititis

Several years ago when Millard was speaking in LaPorte, Indiana, a woman named Gail Elliott drew him aside to tell him about some "bug" her husband Bill had caught. "Ever since," she said, "he's been touring slum neighborhoods and talking incessantly about 'decent housing,' 'biblical economics,' and 'God's people in need.' And he's been doing strange things like digging out his tool box he hasn't touched for years, polishing his hammer, and oiling his wrench. And besides that," she went on, "he's started spending time praying and filling out forms—something called an application for affiliation with Habitat for Humanity."

"He's just got Infectious Habititis," Millard responded.

Before long, Gail realized she had caught the "bug," too. She and Bill worked hard to help start a Habitat for Humanity project in their local area. For vacations, they took trips to Habitat celebrations in Kansas City and Atlanta. Now they are both trying to infect others with Habititis. They do so because of the joy this "infection" has brought them, and they want to share it with as many people as possible.

Some people may have the notion that helping those in need for little or no pay is unpleasant, depressing, or perhaps even a waste of time. This may be true to an extent because any time one becomes involved with the poor there are sure to be some discomforts and problems.

However, if you want to experience moments of sheer joy and downright fun, there is nothing better for the heart, mind, and soul than to get involved in helping some individual or family less fortunate than yourself.

At Habitat for Humanity, we have seen work parties from churches, colleges, and communities shovel dirt, lay blocks, nail shingles, and get sweaty, mosquito-bitten, sunburned, and dirty. But, afterward, they go home exclaiming that it was the best time in their whole lives. Living together in Christian community, praying, working, and sharing meals together, can build not only houses but relationships and understanding as well. Most work party participants immediately start making plans for the next project.

Jimmy Carter often comments about the joy he and Rosalynn experience in working as volunteers for Habitat for Humanity. "The most rewarding and joyful activity we are engaged in," is the way he expresses it.

Paid Nothing?

Some people, though, find it difficult to comprehend why anyone would volunteer to help build houses without getting paid. Remember the man in Charlotte who couldn't believe all those people were working for nothing? A similar episode occurred two years later at the Carter Work Project in Philadelphia. A couple of police officers came by the construction site early one evening. They wanted to know if it was true that the people working there were unpaid volunteers.

When Shirley Schaeffer, the local Habitat affiliate president, assured them that that was indeed the case, they suggested that Habitat could at least pay $10 a day. Shirley responded by telling the officers that the builders really didn't want any money.

Why then, they wanted to know, were the people doing that sort of thing? Why did they want to work for free?

She told the officers the people were there because of a religious motivation.

"What kind of a religion is it?" they asked. "Is it some kind of religion we have here in America?"

She said, "Yes, it's Presbyterian, Episcopalian, Baptist, United Methodist, Catholic, Disciples of Christ, Mennonite, and United Church of Christ, to name a few."

They walked away, genuinely perplexed.

A return to the idea of neighbor helping neighbor, people helping people, and "doing unto others as you would have them do to you" is exciting, refreshing, and "catching." Habitat for Humanity embodies these ideals and has given thousands of people everywhere opportunities to employ them.

New Definition of Success

In his inaugural address, President George Bush talked about a new definition for success. He said, "From now on in America any definition of a successful life must include serving others." In 1989, Habitat for Humanity was one of twenty volunteer organizations or individuals to receive the special President's Volunteer Action Award. We did some quick figuring and to our surprise estimated that Habitat for Humanity currently had more than 70,000 regular volunteers in the United States and thousands more abroad.

We chose two of our volunteers who personified the "Habitat volunteer" to receive the award from President Bush—Amy Parsons and Rick Hathaway. Amy, having already been a Habitat volunteer in Americus for several years, had just completed a three-month, 25,500-mile tour with Christian pop singer Amy Grant. She and another volunteer, Nancy Claussen, drove a van loaded with Habitat promotional materials to fifty-six cities and set up displays in lobbies of concert halls. Because of the appealing "plugs" Amy Grant gave Habitat from the stage, the two Habitat volunteers talked with thousands during intermissions and following the shows.

Rick, an outstanding young engineer from Lynn, Massachusetts, had directed the house-building portion of the 1,200-Mile House-Raising Walk '88. He and his crews worked on the 154 houses from Portland, Maine to Atlanta, Georgia. He and Amy Parsons represented us proudly at the White House as President Bush presented them with the Presidential Award.

Who Would Do It This Way?

Diane Nunnelee, former director of volunteer services, described the crucial role of volunteers in Habitat's ministry:

"In the way the world works, who can imagine entrusting

the construction of homes, the administration of projects, the recruitment of volunteers, the management of contributions, or the entire House-Raising Walk project to people who ask little or nothing in material reward?

"But then Habitat is not about doing things the way the world does. Perhaps that is why people volunteer. Habitat is an arena of servanthood. It affirms gifts and skills offered in love. It is a witness to the truth of the gospel promise that 'as you give, so you shall receive.'

"What we do know is that Habitat needs volunteers, and not just for the work they accomplish. Each new volunteer brings a new vitality, a new spirit of willingness, new questions, and new answers. They keep us newly focused on who we are and who it is God calls us to be, as they demand of Habitat a consistency in being who we say we are. And they bring a willingness to accept people of diverse backgrounds and beliefs, learning from one another, incarnating through service together the body of Christ in the world."

Putting Themselves in the Offering Plate

Volunteers are everything to Habitat for Humanity. Even before Habitat was formed, hundreds of volunteers played a vital role in the development of the Partnership Housing Program at Koinonia. And in the years since, volunteers have been the backbone of this international ministry.

The work of Habitat for Humanity has literally moved on the shoulders of volunteers. People from all walks of life, from all over the United States and many other countries, have offered themselves as volunteers to lend a helping hand to this mushrooming venture of faith. Some work a day or two. Others volunteer for a month, two months, a year, or longer.

Of the more than 200 positions at our international headquarters in Americus, over half are filled by volunteers receiving only free lodging and utilities and a small stipend for food and other personal needs. Many of these volunteers, especially retired people, receive no stipend. In our American, Canadian, Australian, and South African affiliated projects, over 90 percent of the construction and administrative work is done by volunteers. Habitat's international volunteers, while receiving a small stipend during their three years of service, commit to raise as much of their own support as possible in order to free up funds for use in building more houses.

In a real sense, Habitat volunteers "put themselves in the offering plate." They donate their time, ideas, and expertise absolutely free or for a small living allowance. This gift of themselves is an enormous contribution to the burgeoning venture of Habitat for Humanity as these dedicated women and men build houses, stuff envelopes, run programs related to special housing needs, take visitors on tours, type letters, write news releases, unstop commodes, and do scores of other jobs.

Habititis Changes Lives, Too

Not only do people work on Habitat projects without pay, some leave well-paying jobs for a time to be full-time Habitat volunteers. Dennis and Vert Miller of Goshen, Indiana, and Ken and Nancy Keefer of Marietta, Pennsylvania, both Mennonite couples, moved to Americus to become Habitat volunteers. They said they came because of a felt need to be of service to others. Dennis and Ken were both skilled builders back home. Vert was adept at office skills and Nancy was responsible for keeping volunteer houses supplied and furnished.

Such volunteers form lasting friendships while they serve. Vert and Dennis became especially close to one particular homeowner family, headed by Hazel Carter, and all but adopted Hazel's grandson, Richard. "Little Richard," they call him. When it came time for Dennis and Vert to return to Indiana, they were expecting their first baby but took Little Richard home with them for a couple of weeks. He had never been out of the state of Georgia before and had the time of his life. And the families still stay in touch.

Al Newkirk is a builder in Americus. Employed by Habitat for Humanity to renovate volunteer houses and construct new buildings, Al goes way beyond the call of duty. When most volunteers and workers leave at five o'clock, Al works on until seven o'clock or even later. On weekends, he volunteers still more overtime without pay. In our "eight-to-five" work-a-day world, Al's quiet, dedicated nature is wonderfully infected with Habititis.

Once we learned of a flight attendant who found it necessary to quit her job due to severe depression. She was spending most of her time lounging on her living room sofa staring at the ceiling or the television. A Habitat project director came to visit her one day and asked to look at her hands. Seeing they were delicate and smooth, she exclaimed, "Why, these hands don't have any calluses! What you need is something to do." She urged her to come work for one day at their local Habitat construction site. The young woman returned time and time again, replacing her depression with Habititis.

Occasionally, a person will get so badly infected with Habititis he or she just walks away from home and job to make a career of Habitat for Humanity. Such a person is Carol Gregory, an elementary school teacher. Millard met her when he spoke in her home town of Ashland, Kentucky, in March 1986. He told her about the Walk to Kansas City and she decided to walk half of the thousand miles—from Americus to Memphis—during her summer break. After she left us, though, she missed the fellowship so much that she rejoined us several days later and completed the Walk.

But she still hadn't had enough of Habitat. So Carol came to Americus as a full-time volunteer, ultimately accepting a permanent staff position to head up the local building and homeowner program. And in September 1989, she took a three-month leave of absence to go to Australia to give a boost to that country's new Habitat for Humanity program.

Helped as Well as Helping

Sometimes it seems Habitat volunteers are helped as much or more than the help they render. In Rochester, New York, a man named Mike saw in a restaurant a poster for Flower City Habitat that said: "God's People In Need Can Still Use A Good Carpenter!" Mike, although in a very drunken condition, took down the phone number and called the Habitat affiliate. He had been in construction until a back injury and alcoholism left him unemployed. But on that day, Mike spoke of his long-buried dreams of forming a training program with unemployed and disadvantaged youth. Soon, he began with increasing regularity to work with youth at the affiliate's job site. When the affiliate had a groundbreaking for two houses on Hollister Street (students from ten area colleges were to frame them in one week), Mike was there ready to work. One morning the AC Spark Plug Division of General Motors hosted a breakfast for local Habitat advisors. Mike came in late, having walked the last several miles after his car broke down. Later that week, singer Amy Grant worked with the students in framing the houses. Mike was there, too.

It wasn't long afterward that Mike was able to admit his alcohol addiction and do something about it. He was able to see that his dream to work with youth would never be fulfilled until some basic changes were made in his own life. It has now been months since Mike has had a drink and he has drafted a proposal for youth job training for the local Habitat board's consideration.

Working and Learning about Each Other

Some volunteers come to Habitat work sites for enjoyment and enrichment, having heard about the great experience of building houses together.

Rollin Handrich of Elkhart County, Indiana, tells of an experience that is fairly universal for Habitat affiliates. As a rule, when a large work group is needed, a local project will contact one or two churches to provide the volunteers. However, in September 1988 the Elkhart affiliate planned to raise the shells of two houses in one day and that would require at least fifty volunteers.

"Since one of the goals of an affiliate is to bring people together who may not otherwise interact, a plan was devised to include as many churches as possible," he said. "I already had fifteen regular volunteers who had signed up early so I needed another thirty-five. I then contacted seven churches and Goshen College and requested no more than six volunteers each. As I expected, we ended up with over forty additional volunteers, so we assigned other work for the extras. It was very exciting to see everyone working together on assigned tasks, spending the day not only building houses, but also making friends with people from other denominations. All had a good time and we met our goal of raising both houses by 5:30 that afternoon."

Age isn't any prerequisite, either. Rollin loves to use retired persons:

"When work needs to be done during the week, I often rely on retired volunteers. I particularly enjoyed a recent workday in which we textured the walls prior to painting. My work group consisted of four retired men, three of whom were over eighty-three years of age. All had helped me before, but never as a group."

In fact, these older volunteers can be outstanding. Willis Bucher of Lancaster, Pennsylvania, is seventy-nine years old and has been infected with Habititis for eight years. Before he retired, he had been a carpenter. As a Habitat volunteer, Willis has worked in Florida, Arizona, Georgia, Nicaragua, and Honduras, as well as with the local Habitat project. In Lancaster, he was an original Habitat board member and was a driving force in building the first house, putting in 400 hours. He has since given hundreds of additional hours as well.

Willis doesn't go anywhere without his Habitat hat or his Habitat bumper sticker on his van. He always has one of Millard's books handy and is ready and able to tell the Habitat story to anyone who will listen.

Cliff Johnson of Waco, Texas, is the same way. Cliff remembers when he couldn't buy a can of oil, and says he was twenty years old before he knew that socks weren't made with the holes already in them. His family used to live in the kind of houses that Habitat homeowners are leaving behind—the kind where, as Cliff says, "you could throw a cat through the cracks in the walls."

But Cliff's motivation, like Willis Bucher's, is that he's "doin' it for the Lord." And what he's doing is a lot. Cliff has donated the labor and materials for the electrical wiring in Waco Habitat houses and plans to keep it up. With good helpers, each house takes about three days of work.

"I've seen the time I couldn't have put a nickel in the pot," Cliff says, "and others helped me. I'm thankful that I now have the health and ability to help other folks."

Rich and Joyce van Weelden of Oscaloosa, Iowa, have been taking groups of volunteers from their church—Central Reformed—to work in the Kansas City, Missouri, Habitat project since 1985. By late 1989, they had led seventeen week-long work groups to that project. Asked why they keep coming back, Joyce said, "Because we care. We want to build houses in order to share Christ with others. I suppose we'll continue to come as long as the Lord provides health for us." (The folks in Kansas City call their Oscaloosa partners "those crazy flying Dutchmen" because of their Dutch names and fast work.)

Another couple, Al and Shirley Mitchell, young retirees from Silver City, New Mexico, came to Americus in the Spring of 1989 to serve as volunteers for three months. During that time, Al and Shirley caught such a strong case of Habititis they returned to their home area and in the next three months told the Habitat story seventy-four times to various churches and other groups. Dozens of people were inspired to join them in forming a Habitat group. In early March, 1990, the Mitchells mailed in an application for Gila Region Habitat for Humanity to become the 449th U.S. Habitat affiliate.

Civic Clubs

Individuals and churches are not the only ones "infected" with Infectious Habititis. Various civic clubs have caught the disease, too. Florida's Port Charlotte Kiwanis Club is a case in point. Their officers began to investigate the need for low-income housing. This involved visits to social agencies, clergy, and needy families. Through Habitat, they annually earmark money in their budget for "Building homes for our neighbors." About forty volunteers shared in the building of their first house. They developed a great camaraderie with each other. Members of the club told us they were delighted to work with the first homeowner, doing everything from cleaning floors to installing shingles on the roof.

Social and Psychological Barriers Torn Down

It is easy to see how people get "hooked" by working in partnership with those in need. Social and psychological barriers are torn down as houses go up and loving friendships develop. Barbara Wilson of Raleigh, North Carolina, had just such an experience while working as a volunteer with the local Habitat group, Habitat for Humanity of Wake County:

"My story really begins after Dorothy Gordon [a new Habitat homeowner] moved in and I went over to take her a 'welcome' meal. I took homemade soup, salad, and muffins. I also took a fresh pot of mums for her new kitchen. When I arrived Dorothy was not home. An unknown man was raking the side yard. He greeted me, as did several neighborhood dogs. He said he had offered to do some yard work for Dorothy. I responded that I was going to leave the food and flowers for Dorothy and her son Greg at the front door. He explained that doing so would not be good because the dogs would surely get the food. He said he sometimes stayed in the house next door (a condemned, boarded-up structure) and would take the food and see that Dorothy got it. I watched as he put my homemade food on the porch of the condemned house and I drove away thinking Dorothy and Greg would never know I had been there.

"I didn't even call Dorothy to see if she got the food but it later struck me—if the stranger from the boarded-up house needed the food more than Dorothy, then my mission was even more complete.

"Dorothy called me the next day to say how much she and Greg enjoyed the soup and the pretty mums which she later planted in her front yard!"

So often, friendships are forged that last long after the final nail is driven and the new owners move in. In South Carolina, Ed Walpole, a Habitat volunteer, looked out a window of his home and saw a tornado coming at full force. He ran to the basement and threw himself on the floor. He could hear glass shattering and wind whipping through the upstairs. The house was devastated. After a few minutes it was all over. Ed got up, surveyed the damage around him, and thanked God he was alive.

When news flashed on television about the tornado damage, Habitat homeowner Pedro Suchil immediately thought about his friends, Betty and Ed Walpole. (Betty was driving home from Charleston when the tornado hit.) The Walpoles were Pedro's Habitat sponsors and he was concerned about them. He called to make sure they had not been hurt and then drove out to see for himself. He insisted that they come and stay in his Habitat house for safety at least for the night. The next morning, he and Mike Ziegelmeyer, Habitat construction coordinator, went out to lend whatever assistance they could. By the end of the day, forty people had come to clean up, board windows, provide food, and just be there to show their love and concern.

Habititis Infects the Very Young

Kindergarten classes have collected pennies to buy doors and windows. Our two youngest daughters, Faith and Georgia, at ages six and three, were whitewashing exterior concrete block walls in Zaire.

A group of neighborhood children cut grass, washed windows, and raked yards to collect money for a playground near dozens of beautiful Habitat homes in the Optimist Park section of Charlotte, North Carolina.

On his fourth birthday, Jonathan Pittman of Tupelo, Mississippi, emptied his piggy bank of its $2.92 and told his mother he wanted to give it to Habitat for Humanity. Jonathan had heard about building houses for the poor from his parents and at Sunday school.

Mrs. Estey's sixth-grade class at Mesarobles School in Hacienda Heights, California, sent a check to Habitat for Humanity headquarters in Americus along with this fine letter from one of the class members:

> . . . *Our class raised $178 by having a bake sale and chipping in part of our allowance. My class had a controversial debate on what we would like to spend the money for. And we came to a conclusion, we decided to buy seven blocks, a toilet, a door, and a wall.* . . .
>
> *Your friend,*
> *Raymond Yu*

No Race, Color, or Creed

And Infectious Habititis is an equal opportunity "disease" that strikes anyone.

At a city-wide fund-raiser luncheon during the Chicago Jimmy Carter Project in 1986, Linda was busy at her table soliciting a contribution for the international headquarters in Americus. We had recently moved into the first two buildings of our new headquarters complex at Habitat and Church streets. The man across the table from Linda was a very successful young African-American businessman who manufactured mini-blinds exactly like ones we needed for our then-barren windows. Linda told him of our need, and he immediately said his company would be glad to furnish all blinds needed for the two buildings, free of charge. When Linda returned to the office a few days later, she sent him an exact count, along with precise measurements. The blinds arrived shortly thereafter, as ordered. They still grace our office windows today.

And so it goes and goes.

The ways in which people are infected with Habititis are as varied as the people themselves. You can tell it from the letters we receive:

> *Guess what! I've caught it! I am so glad about the way Jesus is unveiling His plan for my life. Habitat is a part of that plan. Day by day is one day closer to the day that Habitat builds its first house for God's people in need in Lima, Ohio. It is exciting! . . .*
>
> *In Christ,*
>
> *Bruce Hilty*

> *I have three daughters (grown), sixteen grandchildren, one great grandchild, and more ideas on the spur of the moment than most folks know what to do with. I've always thought I should and could find a place to use them and Habitat is my current outlet (about ten years with Habitat). I know the national average for an enthused*

volunteer is five years, and I must admit that is about the time I got my second wind, but I still stay enthused. . . .

Sharon Brown

Farmland, Indiana

The first project Jack and I worked on approximately ten years ago was Immokalee, Florida. I recall coming out of People's Chapel on Sunday morning to find a basket of green peppers at our trailer door—a gift from a migrant worker whose family was soon to become a recipient of a Habitat home. This was his way of saying "Thank you."

Another year we had the privilege of working on Mamie Brown's new home. I remember the good feeling I had as we shared a potluck meal together, with Jeff Moreno (a homeowner) cooking delicious barbecue ribs. With the ethnic mixture in Immokalee, and volunteers from various states and Canada, we obviously had different shades of skin and came from various backgrounds, but we were all united in the love of Christ.

Returning three years later to Immokalee, Jack and I were driving down a street and saw Mamie Brown walking with a young boy toward Lake Trafford to try their luck at fishing. As we slowed to say "hello," Mamie immediately shouted, "I know you—you helped build my home!" How very special she made me feel that she remembered.

Lois Wolters

Columbus, North Carolina

As one of our volunteers, Chris Dykes, shared in devotions one morning in Americus near the end of his term of service in 1989: "You and I are in University right now. We are at Habitat U.—Americus Campus. There are hundreds of other campuses in North America and overseas with thousands of undergrads currently enrolled.

"There are no graduates from this school. No one ever graduates from Habitat U. We may come and go, but we'll not receive our diploma until poverty housing is eliminated from the face of the earth; and when that happens, I'll bet Habitat for Humanity opens up a new department, and starts teaching about a different problem."

Homeowners Infected

Habititis also infects the homeowners just as much. Marilyn Walker of Charlotte, North Carolina, decided to collect money to help the local Habitat affiliate raise $1.5 million. Marilyn, a high school dropout and a single mother of three, said, "Habitat turned me around. I figured if Jimmy Carter could pick up a shovel and hammer, why couldn't I help?"

Having moved from a dilapidated rental house, Marilyn was anxious to show appreciation for her new three-bedroom home. She wanted to help but didn't know exactly how. She attended a meeting and found out about the need to raise money.

"I had never tried to raise money," she said. "But I figured the neighborhood I work in is real nice—big houses, nice cars—and maybe I could get some people to contribute. I was a little scared, but I figured they can't do nothing but say 'Yes' or 'No.'"

At that time, Marilyn was cleaning house and taking care of two children—a two-year-old and a ten-year-old. She asked her employers if they would mind if she went door-to-door in the neighborhood when taking the girls out for their morning and afternoon strolls. They thought it was a great idea.

Marilyn carried Habitat pamphlets and knocked on doors. By the end of the first day, she had collected $67 in checks and cash. She excitedly called the local Habitat office and reported that she was "shooting" for $100.

The children got real excited, too. Marilyn still laughs about the time one lady asked how much she wanted and the younger child quickly spoke up and said, "Five dollars, please." Marilyn met her $100 goal, then upped it to $200, then $300. Eventually she raised nearly a thousand dollars.

Give and You Shall Receive

For the person infected with Habititis, giving always means receiving, too. A fundamental nerve is being hit with the opportunity Habitat offers and more and more people are responding—and they keep responding. We hope Infectious Habititis will never run its course.

Nancy Olson of Duluth, Minnesota, wrote us about her case of Habititis and how she helped start a Habitat project in her area:

> I agreed to coordinate the Sunday morning Adult Studies for my church in the fall of 1987. I thought it would be a kick to invite a Habitat representative to Duluth to speak. My husband and I had been supporters of Habitat for Humanity for a couple of years but little did we realize how deeply enmeshed we would get from that cavalier invitation. There was nothing enticing in the invitation. We offered no money, no gas allowance, and no hotel, just a bed in our basement. I laughed, throwing it in the mail box. Who would accept such a crummy offer?
>
> Ten days later, Jim Carr, the volunteer coordinator for Habitat Midwest, called and asked, "When do you want me? I'm coming for free." We settled on a day. . . .
>
> Immediately, my Lutheran guilt set in. Jim was coming for free, for just one church. He had to be better utilized than that. But as I asked other pastors if they could use a speaker that weekend, they uniformly said, "No . . . , but wouldn't it be neat to have an affiliate here in Duluth?" It sounded wonderful to me, but I knew I wasn't going to do it. I was a mother of three and had great responsibilities.
>
> But God had infected me with Habititis. Throughout the next several months, complete strangers called and asked: "Is it true you're forming a Habitat affiliate in Duluth?" I could never figure out how they had

heard it. I kept responding that I would try to have a public meeting but I certainly was not forming an affiliate. Through the mysterious grapevine I heard about a couple, Ray and Phyllis Miller, who were interested in Habitat. I called their house several times with no success. Finally, I decided to try one last time and the phone was answered. The person explained that the Millers were out of town, but agreed to take a message. When I told him about the public meeting I was trying to put together for Habitat, he gasped and replied, "Do you know where they are? They're away for two months building Habitat houses in Austin, Texas. I'm here watering the plants and decided to answer the phone this one time!" He left an ecstatic message for the Millers.

Shortly thereafter we connected. Phyllis and I contacted all the media, every ministerial group we could, city government and housing groups, individual churches, anyone we could think of. . . .

So what happened? Over forty people came to our meeting. Jim Carr told the Habitat story. Within one and a half hours we had a steering committee. I'm the president and Phyllis is chairing the Speakers Bureau.

It can happen that easily. Catching Infectious Habititis may be the most fun and fulfillment you've ever had, and we pray you'll catch it just like Nancy did, if you're not already infected.

Write or call your local Habitat affiliate,[1] or write Habitat for Humanity International, Americus, Georgia, 31709–3498 and any questions you might have will be answered. We'll expose you to Habititis and get you started helping a host of others eliminate poverty housing and homelessness from the face of the earth.

6

The Man with the Land

The famous American humorist Will Rogers once said that everybody is ignorant, only on different subjects.

Of course, he's right, but what he didn't say is that the opposite is true, too. Everybody is smart about something and everybody can make a contribution in one way or another to the community and world we live in. We all have resources, financial and otherwise, which can be used to help solve whatever problem is confronting us.

In the work of Habitat for Humanity, we are always trying to link up people and resources to get the job done. And we learned a long time ago that the best way to get what you need is to ask for it. The Bible tells us to *ask.* It does not say, "Engage in wishful thinking and you will receive." It says, "Ask and you will receive."

And when you ask, things happen.

No Land

One night we attended a Habitat meeting in north Georgia. Arriving a few minutes early, we had an opportunity to visit informally with several of the leaders of the newly forming group. They told us they felt they were making good progress. They had gotten incorporated. Committees had been formed. Some money had been raised. There was only one problem— they didn't have any land. They had searched and searched, but just could not find any building sites. So when Millard began speaking that night, he talked about the land problem.

"You don't have any land, I understand," Millard said. "I find that a bit strange. When we drove into town a while ago, I saw land everywhere. It was on the right side of the road and the left. Even the road was built on land.

"The Bible teaches us that the earth is the Lord's. That includes your city. Most of you here this evening are strangers to me. I don't know you personally. I don't know about your finances, abilities, or possessions. But, I do know that you've got land. I don't know who's got what, but I know you've got it, and God knows, too. It all belongs to Him anyway.

"So, what I want tonight is for the person who has some of God's property that could be used by your new Habitat project to come up and let us know who you are. We'll solve the land problem right quick."

When Millard finished speaking, a distinguished, silver-haired gentleman came forward and said, "I'm the man with the land. While you were talking about it, my wife almost poked my ribs out. I'll have my lawyer make the deed out next week."

A few weeks later, Millard was visiting a new Habitat project in south Georgia. The project leaders said essentially the same thing those in north Georgia had. Everything seemed to be falling into place except for the land. They just could not find any land.

Millard again asked for the man with the land. And, again, a man came up to say that he was the man with the land in that town.

Shortly thereafter, Millard was on a speaking tour in California. A local Habitat project had just completed its first three houses. The group was anxious to build more, but—guess what?—no land. In a big public gathering at a high school, Millard told the two Georgia "man with the land" stories. And, sure enough, when he ended the speech, up came a man who said he had a large tract of land, possibly enough for seventeen houses, that he would donate to the project.

Such responses come again and again. In August 1989, once more Millard was on a speaking tour, this time in the Northwest. In a session with a new Habitat affiliate in Bend, Oregon, project leaders prior to the community meeting said the same thing—everything was in place but they couldn't find any land. So, you can imagine what Millard told them in the meeting. But this time he said it was about time for a woman with land to come forward, knowing for a fact that men did not own all the land.

At the end of the meeting, no one came forward. Not a woman. Not a man. No one, which was a little discouraging. And, especially so, because the crowd that night was very large—several hundred people—and "land" was written all over many faces.

But then Millard went home with the hosts for the evening and while they were enjoying some refreshments before going to bed, they told him, "Perhaps we are the people with the land. We have a large lot that we could give to the project."

The next morning, at a coffee hour at the Habitat office, a lady walked in and handed Millard a real estate sales contract. She explained that she was the lady with the land and that the two lots described in that contract would be donated to the local project. She smiled, patted Millard on the back, and left.

Overall Feeling of Joy

That is the way it happens. People have different stories for why they are giving. The Rev. Robert Sulanke, in giving land to the new Muncie, Indiana, Habitat project back in 1987, perhaps explained best what the overall feeling of joy is:

"First, after reading *No More Shacks!* and feeling the good spirit of the Muncie group, I wanted to be in the movement of Habitat for Humanity. This gift is an expression of being 'on board.'

"Second, Muncie has been home for my wife and me forty years. Life has been good to us and we wanted to give back something in gratitude. Helping to build new homes for needy people is one way of being grateful.

"Third, there are two texts in the Bible which are a constant challenge to me. One is the response of John the Baptist to the people who came to the Jordan River asking, 'What then shall we do?' His answer was, 'He who has two coats, let him share with him who has none.' We have a nice home on a lot. These five lots can help some other families have homes.

"The other text is Matthew 25. Speaking of those who shared food, water, clothes, and deeds of kindness, Jesus said, 'As you did it to one of the least of these my brothers, you did it to me.'"

Overseas Land

Overseas, land is often a problem, especially in heavily populated metropolitan areas. Habitat had learned about the deplorable living conditions of a group of very low income families on the northern fringe of Metro Manila in the Philippines.

The biggest problem was securing land for the 150 families who desperately needed housing. Then, a partnership arrangement with Philippine Christian University and a local cooperative was formed that gave control of a five-acre tract of land so that Habitat houses could be built for the poor families.

Little Ripples of Answered Prayer

Sometimes, land is not the problem in a Habitat project, but something else is.

Early in 1988, Clint McCoy of Wayne County, New York, Habitat told a youth group in Connecticut they could come in June to work for a week but that they should pray that the site would be ready for them.

By mid-May, everything was in place except for a mason. Land had been given, surveying and site preparation donated, legal fees waived, and house plans provided at half cost. But, no mason. They had been looking for someone who would give a price break or do the work free, but, with good weather approaching, all masons, it seemed, were already committed to other jobs.

Finally, just three days before the date set for putting in the footers, a mason was finally located. This man's scheduled job had fallen through at the last minute. Clint says he was probably the only mason in the county who was available at that time. The mason took the job and said he'd be willing to work with volunteers.

The next week, as the block work was about to begin, Clint got a call from the block company saying that they didn't have credit information on Habitat for Humanity, so the blocks couldn't be sent to the work site. A credit check was set in motion but, in the meantime, the blocks were sent to the site on the good name of the mason.

Things just seem to work out, over and over. The Holston Habitat project in northeastern Tennessee needed a concrete finisher and a sign painter. In a speech to a church group, President Jo Morrison told about the two special needs. In the group was a visitor who was a skilled concrete finisher. He volunteered. Then a retiree who had a flair for painting said he'd love to help. Jo calls these kinds of incidents, "the Lord's little ripples of answered prayer," and that's a wonderful way to put it.

Over and over, these little ripples flow over us. Things fall in place. It's always exciting to watch what happens.

Divine Engineer

Sometimes these ripples are surprising. Lee County Habitat for Humanity in Fort Myers, Florida, tells of one such unusual ripple. An all-volunteer crew started early one Saturday morning assembling pre-fabricated walls, door frames, and trusses—all rough work to be completed by late that afternoon. Unfortunately, when time came to set the roof trusses, they simply would not fit. With half of the trusses already incorrectly in place, it was soon determined that no manner of recalculation or relocation would solve the problem.

About that time, a rather nondescript passerby stopped and looked over the situation. After a minute or two of thoughtful observation, he asked if he could survey the scene in more detail. Because everyone was so frustrated by this time, the man was hardly noticed as he scurried nimbly up the framework and examined the layout. He soon came down and gave all the dejected volunteers a jolt. He explained a detailed, but basic solution to the seemingly insoluble problem. The volunteers quickly set about doing just as he suggested, and his plan worked to perfection. And then they noticed that their "Divine Engineer" had vanished.

Donating Whatever You Do Well

Often, money is a missing ingredient in a local Habitat affiliate. Sometimes the answer comes in small amounts and sometimes very big ones. During 1988, Habitat of Rhode Island had raised approximately $33,000. At the beginning of 1989, they set a goal to at least double the previous year's accomplishments. With that goal in mind, the Board of Directors met in early January. Several guests attended the meeting. They were introduced and invited to contribute to the discussions. Two of the guests, a husband and wife, asked quite a few questions about the cost of a duplex, and how the construction would be done. Then these folks quietly left the meeting a few minutes early, handing a check to the fund-raising chairman on the way out. As the meeting was about to close, the chairman announced the amount of the contribution—$30,000.

Sometimes, an entire organization comes forth to help out in a dramatic way with all kinds of resources—financial, management skills, and expertise in construction—to pull off a dramatic event. In October 1988, the Nashville-Middle Tennessee Home Builders Association teamed up with Nashville Habitat to build an entire house in a day. Two hundred professional workers donating their time, thirty suppliers making generous donations, and a lot of prayer combined to put up a 972-square-foot house. In a record twenty-two hours the house was finished and occupied.

The event was such a positive experience for everyone involved that it was repeated a year later. We were there for the building of the second house. It was completed in twenty hours and fifty-five minutes.

In May 1989, Tedd Benson, one of the founders of the Timber Framers Guild, organized a blitz of two houses in partnership with York, Pennsylvania, Habitat for Humanity. Timber framers from forty states and four foreign countries descended upon the little town of Hanover, near York, to put up the two houses in just three days.[1]

Just Yourself

Sometimes all "the man" (or the woman) has is just himself (or herself). And yet even that can be dramatic.

Alan Derrick literally gave himself to Huntsville, Alabama, Habitat for Humanity when he climbed up on a billboard in that city in November 1988. He vowed to remain until enough money, labor, and materials for four houses—or $100,000—was contributed. He also wanted to raise awareness about Habitat's work. The thirty-two-year-old owner of a construction company said, "I can get down from here when this is over and go home, but a lot of people can't go back to a home."

Alan finally descended from his lofty perch after six and a half days in the wake of tornado warnings. He had raised $60,000 in cash, pledges, and materials.

Alan's dramatic fund-raising idea inspired another man, Jack Ramsey of Jackson, Mississippi, to the same heights for Habitat. He climbed up on a billboard in November 1989, stayed for a week, and raised $150,000 in money and materials for the Jackson Habitat affiliate.

We're constantly amazed at what one person with whatever talent he or she has can do. Stan George, a retired Presbyterian pastor from San Clemente, California, is one of those creative people. Since 1987, he has been aggressively raising funds for Habitat for Humanity through a group of people he calls "George Partners." These people help him and his wife, Helen, match all first-time gifts of up to $1,000 from individuals to the three groups he supports.[2] In this way, Stan is introducing thousands of new people to Habitat and to getting them "hooked" on solving the problem of inadequate shelter and homelessness.

To promote his work, Stan rides his motorcycle across the country, speaking to churches and other groups along the way. He sprinkles his speeches with good humor, but he has a very serious message. He wants people to put their faith to work and make a difference in the world. He surely is making a difference in Habitat for Humanity.

Sometimes It's a Stage, Sometimes Salad Dressing

And then there are people who have a literal stage from which to "give," and they do. Many outstanding entertainers have helped Habitat over the years—Bob Hope, Willie Nelson, Ben Vereen, Ken Medema, Richie Havens, the Indigo Girls, and others.

Popular singer/songwriter Amy Grant started promoting Habitat for Humanity during her "Lead Me On" tour in 1988–1989. She and her husband, Gary Chapman, worked on Habitat building sites in Rochester, New York, and Birmingham, Alabama. In her concert in Pittsburgh in November 1988, Amy told over 8,000 of her fans, "I'm coming to realize something as I get older. It's easy to ignore the problems in the world that surround us and say, 'The government will take care of it,' or 'The big church on the corner will take care of it.' But, for me, it's becoming more important to make my faith more than just words—to get in there and do something about those problems, like building a house for someone. That's why I'm endorsing Habitat for Humanity."

Buddy Greene, well-known harmonica virtuoso, not only gave a benefit concert during the House-Raising Walk in 1988, as well as contributing financially, but he also came to Americus in 1989 to do another benefit concert.

Radio personality and best-selling author Garrison Keillor did a benefit concert for Tallahassee, Florida, Habitat for Humanity in March 1986. In addition, he is a generous contributor to the work. Paul Newman, the famous actor, narrated a video program for Charlotte, North Carolina, Habitat for Humanity. Also, for several years he has given generously from his company, Newman's Own, well known for salad dressing and other food products. (In January 1990, we received a gift of $275,000 from the company.)

The most interesting gift of all, concerning stages, was the gift of a stage itself. In September 1988, Billy Graham held a crusade in Rochester, New York. When the crusade ended, the

Billy Graham Organization donated the stage to Habitat for Humanity; it was disassembled and its timber was used to help build two houses.

Always It's Your Heart

The greatest gift, of course, that anyone can give to Habitat for Humanity, or any other Christian ministry, is not land, or money, or time, or a special skill or talent, as important as all those things are. The greatest gift that can possibly be given is one's heart. Many people have done that over the years and this is the primary reason why Habitat has experienced such phenomenal growth. Your heart is touched as you touch others. And you cannot help but be changed by what happens.

The story of a Haitian pastor in a small village in the interior of that country is the best example of "giving a heart" that we have ever known. The pastor's name is Boukan Tilus, and he is a Baptist pastor of a mission, as well as president of the Habitat for Humanity board in Dumay.

We'll let overseas Volunteer Lance Cheslock tell the story in his own words:

> Once, while sitting on Pastor Boukan's porch, I approached him about the homeowner selection for the next three houses that were to be built in the zone where he lived. I knew that he and several committee members were considering about a dozen applicants, and one of the applicants concerned me—a man who was a minister of another church in Galet, the same village where Pastor Boukan's Baptist church was located. Even though the title 'minister' assumes a man or woman of God, this man had a reputation for being one of the most vicious people in the area.
>
> The minister claimed for years that Pastor Boukan's Baptist mission was built on land that really belonged to him. The title said otherwise, but he kept dragging Pastor Boukan to court over and over, with no success. So finally this man resorted to more vicious attacks. The man was also a member of the ruthless

squad of 'secret police,' and proudly wore his uniform to harass Pastor Boukan and his family, stoning his house, beating up his children, intimidating his wife, even resorting to voodoo designed to bring tragic death to Pastor Boukan and his children. One voodoo ritual was performed in their back yard at midnight, and though Pastor Boukan was aware of what was happening, he was too afraid to do anything. It was all just a relentless barrage of hate that seemed to have no rational roots.

Finally, the minister was stripped of his power after the 1986 revolution disbanded the secret police, and much of his harassment of Pastor Boukan and his family lost its intensity.

Then I found out that Pastor Boukan and his subcommittee had already made their three choices for Habitat housing. One of the choices was this man.

I was *outraged!* How could he pick that guy after all the stories he had told me about him?

He simply looked up at me, confused, and said, "Lance, have you ever seen that man's house?" He gestured off toward the bean field . . . . "That man's living conditions are horrible! After considering all of the applicants, he was definitely the first choice." Here we were, our project always having difficulties with house payments, and Pastor Boukan was choosing that louse. It seemed absolutely unreasonable.

"Pastor Boukan," I asked, "don't you think that someone of his character is going to be problematic when it comes time to pay for the house?"

Pastor Boukan seemed as if he knew not where I was coming from. He said, "Lance, you've never seen that man's house. He has six children. Come, let me show it to you." And with that he led me back to the field where the man lived.

As we walked, Pastor Boukan told me he had some verses he wanted to share with me, and from memory he quoted me Exodus 23:3–5 [NASB]. He prefaced it all by saying, "Lance, I'll tell you why I don't consider the past." Then he quoted, "'[N]or shall you be partial to a poor man in his dispute. If you meet your enemy's ox or his donkey wandering away, you shall surely return it to him. If you see the donkey of one who hates you lying helpless under its load, you shall refrain from leaving it to him, you shall surely release it with him. . . . '" After he finished quoting, he said, "The man does need a house; it's that simple."

He was right about the house. Part of the scanty structure was on the verge of collapse, and the rotten roofing grass testified to the leaky, wet nights the man and his family must have experienced.

On the day we began building the house, the man found Pastor Boukan there with a pick in his hand, as well as Boukan's adopted son. The first sight of the three caused me to weep. Pastor Boukan was serious about his convictions! I got hold of myself after a moment and grabbed a shovel and went to work. The group was pretty silent that day, and it was obvious emotions were tense. I imagine the minister was confused by Pastor Boukan's response, but in spite of those tensions, the group worked really hard and finished early.

Pastor Boukan certainly humbled me through this experience. His love in the face of hate still astounds me. I can't say, unfortunately, that the minister has quit harassing Pastor Boukan and his family, for the ugliness continues. I think if I were to do what Pastor Boukan did, I would do it as a "necessary" act to get the man to quit the harassment. However, I don't think that Pastor Boukan had any motive whatsoever. His reason was that it was the right thing to do, for he did not calculate the results of his strategy. He just simply acted, and acted in faith. This story may seem to have a sad ending, given the hardness of his enemy's heart. Yet I am drawn to the joy of realizing Pastor Boukan's unselfish heart.

An unselfish heart!

That's what it takes to be a man or a woman with the land.

A concrete finisher who donates his time to pour concrete for a family he doesn't even know. A young businessman leaving his construction company for a week to sit high on a big billboard to plead for money for the poor. A couple with land or money willing to give it to help others. But, without a doubt, it takes the biggest unselfish heart of all to build a house for your enemy. Come to think of it, that is the very essence and the heart of the gospel, isn't it? The unselfish heart in the face of any situation is definitely the very heart of Habitat, too.

7

Letters from International Partners

My three years with Habitat as an overseas partner are coming to a close.

There have been some hard times, sad times, and lonely times, but there have also been times of joy, peace, and of learning and growth. . . ."

These lines are from a letter written by International Partner Bret Stein, who served in Peru and Bolivia. And his feelings are typical of those of other Habitat for Humanity International Partners.

Previously called "Overseas Volunteers," "International Partners" is a new title which is more descriptive of these dedicated people who commit themselves to work in a sponsored project abroad for three years or more. And being International Partners isn't easy even before they leave the United States. The first three years include eleven weeks in the International Training Program at Habitat headquarters, followed by one to two months of fund-raising prior to departure.

So, you can see that being an International Partner requires a very high level of commitment. Anyone who has visited, lived, or worked in developing countries can understand the sacrifices, frustrations, and struggles experienced by International Partners. Doubtless, there are joys and many benefits, as Bret described above. But it takes mountains of faith, dedication, compassion, and strong character even to attempt such a personal venture.

And it goes without saying that many of the International Partners could write a book themselves.

In this chapter, we want to share excerpts from some of the letters we receive from International Partners.[1] What they tell us of their experiences speaks volumes about the hardships but also the joy of building Habitat houses around the world.

Getting There

Sometimes just getting to their assigned location is an ordeal. But once there, not only pain and joy are found, but also humor:

> Terry and Michele Finseth
> Lata, Solomon Islands
>
> In August [1987] our family left Honiara by ship for the island of Malaita bound for a small obscure village called Harusou. The voyage took all night through a passage of water known to be one of the roughest in the world. . . . I [Michele] got seasick before we even left the harbor! We were down in the hold of the ship (along with floor-to-ceiling boxes, 101 cockroaches, and *heat*) where the ride was supposed to be the calmest! During the night we could feel the boat pitching and rolling—finally Terry got sick enough to go up on deck to spend the rest of the night hanging onto the railing for dear life! At dawn I awoke and went up on deck to a sight I will never forget—the ship was slowly making its way through a lagoon— there was beautiful tropical forest on either side with villages scattered along the shores. Out from the villages came canoes full of people to greet us; some came to tether alongside the ship momentarily to take goods off or put them on. The sun was coming up over the trees and the air was misty. I thought I was in the middle of a movie! . . .
>
> Our journey has not only taken us 7,000 miles from home, but deep into the heart of a new culture

and many learning experiences. At first it seemed as if we learned something new almost daily, but as time has gone on and we've settled in more we've been given the opportunity to put into practice what we've learned.

Many months this year have been spent in the struggle of understanding—and waiting (and waiting, and waiting!). Each month we felt sure this would be the month our milling permit [giving permission to cut trees for lumber] would arrive. We decided that the phrase, "No shirt, no shoes, no service," takes on a whole new connotation here in the Solomons: No one wears shirts, no one wears shoes, and no one gives any service.

In the meantime, we devoted our time and energies to other kinds of building—building of systems (to run the project efficiently), the building of understanding (there's much teaching to be done), and most importantly, the building of relationships.

. . . [T]he lottery was held to decide the building order of the first eight houses. It was so exciting to watch the faces of those homeowners as their names were drawn. Especially the face of Matthew Melake, who passed out after overdosing on betel nut just prior to the drawing! When we inquired as to his whereabouts, people explained, "Betel nut, hem i killum hem!" [Betel nuts are chewed all through the South Pacific. They can produce severe drowsiness or even loss of consciousness if taken in excess.]

Climate

Sometimes, the climate is the ordeal:

Donna and David Minich
Kusip, Papua New Guinea

September brought the BIG rains—two months late, but we've gotten the feel of what being "rained in" means. The road washed out; luckily we had just gotten a month's supply of food, so were all set to sit tight—all except for the laundry . . . and that's a whole different story! We were reminded of the Great Lakes winters that we both grew up in and being "snowed-in." The Habitat work didn't slow up a bit— rain or shine, there's always plenty to do. At the first glimmer of sun, the village men investigate the road and proceed to dig out. . . .

We've dealt with head lice, fleas, amoebic dysentery, an abscessed tooth, ear infections, rashes, skin infections, and flu bugs. Every minute scratch must be attended to or it quickly develops into a full-blown tropical ulcer. So, with our kids, there is usually some kind of ailment or need for minor first aid. I [Donna] really can't say it's more dangerous here—the dangers are just different.

We've certainly experienced hardships and adversities before, but this has to at least have been the most unusual setting. We thank God for such an interesting life and for allowing us to revel in receiving plastic pants, Kool Aid, and herbal mosquito repellent!

Culture

And sometimes, the culture is a source of frustration and also challenge.

David and Donna explain:

Papua New Guinea is unique in the world because of the 700-plus different indigenous languages and dialects spoken here. Each of these language groups has its own distinct identity and customs which enhance the rich cultural heritage and diversity found in PNG. For example, the ways of our Numanggang-speaking people here in the Kusip River area are different from the customs of the folks who live at the bottom of the mountain or even further up the Kusip!

There are some things, though, that do run similarly throughout the country. One of the most widely noted cultural traits of PNG is the "wantok system" or "one-talk" system. Not only is there very strong and unyielding (sometimes unjustifiable) loyalty to your family line, but also to the others from your language group. There are some wonderful aspects of this in terms of community cooperation and the lack of a need for a welfare system. Each group looks out for its own and no individual goes hungry or without a place to live, unless the group as a whole is suffering or an individual has been shamed in some way and turned out from the group. There are also difficulties with the system, too—for instance, if you should marry outside of your language group and have to mesh two different and deeply entrenched sets of customs. Talk about in-law problems!

There have been conflicts in our committee meetings as David has been reprimanded for spending time with outsiders and telling them about Habitat. David has calmly and persistently resisted by stating his Christian convictions and the ideals of Habitat. He constantly reminds people that if we, Millard Fuller, or other Christians held this belief, *no one* in PNG would have Habitat houses. Habitat is a system of "helpim helpim" (everyone helping each other) and we are all wantoks in God's world.

Christmas Gift

International Partners always find holidays in their adopted countries to be unusual. Sometimes they have fantastic experiences:

Karen Foreman
Mbandaka, Zaire

In Zaire, Christmas [1987] was a time to gather with Habitat volunteers from the region and for missionary friends to celebrate. . . . On Christmas Eve while we were . . . discussing celebration plans for the next day, there was a loud knocking at the door. My sentinel burst in exclaiming that the project bike had been impounded by the police because he had been driving it without a light.

Being arrested in Zaire was an almost weekly occurrence and was usually resolved only with the payment of a bribe prompted by the words, "Do you have something for me, Madame?" Almost all the vehicles on the road were without lights, so this incident looked to be another trumped-up excuse for the local police to make some extra money.

We went in search of the bike. To our amused dismay, we found three policemen on different bikes which had all been commandeered (because they had no lights, of course) and were now being used by the officers as transportation back to the station. After we attempted dialogue with the officers, they invited us to come down to the station and tell our story to the captain.

Once at the station, a makeshift shed with a single light bulb overhead, I implored the captain to return our bike to us. I also explained that we were working with Habitat to build decent shelter with those of their people who need it. "Besides," I exclaimed with sudden inspiration, "it's Christmas and you should give us a gift."

"Ha!" the captain replied. "You are the ones who should give us a gift." At this, the other policemen exploded into laughter.

Dismayed, I thought my plan had backfired and we would have to pay the rather expensive bribe after all. Then I hit upon a creative idea. I told the captain that, yes, I would give him and his men a gift, the very best gift they had ever received. I assured them it would be more powerful and productive than they could imagine. Intrigued, but still suspicious, the captain asked, "What is this wonderful gift?"

I replied by shaking each officer's hand and saying, "Citoyen, [Citizen] I will pray for you tonight."

Stunned at first, they soon erupted into boisterous laughter again. Slapping their thighs and shaking their heads, they nodded for us to take the bike and be gone. Bonnie Watson and I took the bike and our story back to the other volunteers. In the spirit of Christmas, we decided to carol as a group for the officers. We again trooped back to the station, bearing cookies and songs to their amazed enjoyment.

Prior to that incident we had experienced a great deal of harassment from the police; however, after that encounter we were never again stopped as targets for harassment or with the expectation to solicit a bribe. . . . When they would stop us they would say, "Oh, you're the ones who came to sing to us!"; then they would laugh and wave us on. This friendship provided a surprising and pleasant gift for the volunteers and workers with the Habitat project.

Unexpected Encounters
The Partners never fail to be amazed at the reality of where they are:

Art Mehaffey
Kinshasa, Zaire

The trip to Lake Tumba was very interesting. This was the first time for me to see this project of more than thirty small villages. Some of the villages are accessible by road, but several can only be reached by water. We visited four of the villages by dugout canoe powered by an outboard motor. During the return trip across the lake, a light rain fell and in the middle we passed within about thirty yards of a hippopotamus crossing the lake. . . .

Marie Dionne
Les Cayes, Haiti

There are a lot of lizards around here and tarantulas also. I met a tarantula face to face a couple of weeks ago and much to my surprise, I didn't totally freak out! I merely dumped him out of my stationery drawer onto the lawn and called out, "Madame, Madame!" Madame Macval, who was nearby, came running to see what the commotion was about. When she saw it, she picked up a rock and slung it at the poor critter. Killed him deader than dead. She's a good shot, that Madame Macval. I had only wanted her to look at it. . . ."

Local Ingenuity

And they write about the hard work of the homeowners in the Habitat projects:

Kathy Ward
Basankusu, Zaire

The project in Basankusu is located on the edge of the Equatorial Rain Forest and the prospective home-owners must clean their land of brush, trees, etc. They also must dig the foundation and make the required number of bricks themselves—lots of hard work for these folks.

Herman Hymerikx
Basankusu, Zaire

To build one house with one family is a story in itself. Only someone who has owned a home might understand. Once a family is in an affordable house the search for food, schooling—everything in their lives—becomes possible. Lives are more productive; there are fewer health problems. What a story to become a homeowner! Beyond the wildest dreams. Some of our "fellowmen" are just hanging on. It's such a small price—to reach out my hand.

Eric Duell
Mexico

. . . In San Pedro Capula—included in our [inauguration] ceremony—the fifty homeowners will choose their house (probably through a raffle) and receive their house keys. The participants have been working incredibly hard. About half of them have already put in over 2,000 hours and they want this once-in-a-lifetime event to be a big hit. They will probably "fest" with a traditional Otami barbecue of about thirty to forty sheep. Not exciting for those who are vegetarians but a real treat for us carnivores!

In Dexthi Alberto, the folks are really "mellow" and they hardly batted an eye when I told them their project had been approved. They weren't able to keep their cool for long and big smiles soon broke out on all their usually stoic faces. They have already begun gathering rocks, sand, and the money for their down payments.

Political Danger
And more than we like to think, the International Partners have to worry about the politics of their adopted country:

Bryan Murphy
Pandyassou, Haiti

Politically, things are calm and business is as usual [November 1988]. I am not scared now, but I was a month ago. The shooting has stopped and the number one prayer of peace has been answered. The situation still is serious, but please be assured that we are safe and in no danger.

Someone once told me that when you become a Christian you are never in the wrong place at the wrong time. I had thought I was in the wrong place at the wrong time when I drove up to the gate of a friend's orphanage and the army wanted to burn an eighteen-year-old kid. I was scared, nervous, and thought they were going to kill that kid as they had many others that day. [This episode describes the violent political situation in Haiti at that time. Many people were shot or burned in the streets simply on suspicion of opposition to the government. Teenage boys were targeted in particular and most commonly doused with fuel and set aflame.]

Yet I still was able to pray during that time that nobody would get hurt, and God did answer that prayer and the thanks go to Him. God is with us, and we are not involved in politics or the problems the government is having, so be assured we do not want to get involved in the political situation. For that reason we are safe and I do not feel we are in any imminent danger and we are not thinking of leaving the country.

Squalid Living Conditions

But they often write of the living conditions, and how bad it can be, even in a developed country like Australia:

Ted Swisher
Sydney, Australia

Australia has an excellent public housing program, but the waiting list is 160,000 families long. If you cannot get into public housing, there is not a good, stable low-cost housing alternative. Sydney is so expensive. A newly selected Habitat family, the Hendersons, are living in a converted chicken barn and paying $520 per month for this dilapidated "house" with a fifty-five-gallon drum for a septic tank and a structure that is being devoured by termites. When the weather is wet, the Hendersons have to pluck mushrooms from the base of their bedroom walls. They've done everything they can to try to find reasonable housing, but they are stuck in a chicken barn.

Bob Williams
General Santos City, Philippines

The city's growth gives promise to those hoping to find work in the boom-town atmosphere. It is generally positive but results in many people coming here who can't find good paying jobs or who can't find a place to live. They end up squatting on government or unused private lands, living in houses which are often made of scrap lumber and woven mat with a thatch roof. Those with a little money may buy tin roofing to do a better job of keeping the rain out. These are the people I find myself serving in my work here.

The families vary in size—many are young couples, some college educated. Invariably the family members are underemployed. I know college graduates who drive small three-wheeled vehicles to transport people or goods as well as school teachers who are vegetable vendors.

The houses, too, vary in form and makeup. One thing they do all have in common: portability. They are meant to be picked up and moved or, at least, easily dismantled. As squatters, these people know that any day they may be forced to move; they cannot afford to invest in permanent building materials which they may have to abandon when the move comes—as it always does.

These past two weeks I helped move four houses which were scheduled to be demolished to make way for a wall that the owner is having built around his property. Visiting the site I saw where there had been houses two days before—now there was a four-foot wall. One house remained to be moved from the site. It had been moved a mere ten feet so the builders could continue their work.

My friends were fortunate—the property owner was fairly understanding of their problem and gave them adequate notice to move. Likewise, the workers were understanding as they tried their best to work around the few remaining homes not directly in the way of the wall. I am certain that as soon as the wall is completed it will become the back of the next group of [homes for] squatters who choose to settle on the narrow strip between there and the roadside.

My friends will not be returning to the site. Inspired by the idea of building decent permanent homes, they formed a cooperative to purchase thirty-six hectares of land which, subdivided, will provide lots for a total of 900 families. The land was far from ready to build on; there is no water or electricity. It is little more than a large field with a few scraggly cotton plants in one corner. But my friends could not afford to wait. A local trucking firm was contracted to carry the houses for only the cost of gas—as time permitted. After almost dropping a house on its corner we decided to jack up the remaining ones and drive the truck out from under them. That was much easier. Today, five families have moved houses to the site where they will wait for a water system and possible financial assistance from Habitat in order to build themselves permanent homes.

Jeff Abbott
Vila-Vila, Peru

The houses in the village were flimsy, insecure fire hazards offering no protection from the winds and fog common along the coast from April to September. Thus in 1987 a project was proposed to and approved by Habitat for Humanity International. Construction was begun in March 1988.

Vila-Vila, prior to the arrival of Habitat, had a reputation for being a den of thieves, drunks, and delinquents. People from Tacna, the capital of the department sixty kilometers away, rarely went to Vila-Vila because of this unfortunate fame. To some extent this reputation was true. Many fishing boats from other ports would arrive at Vila-Vila to unload and sell their catch, their crews would go ashore to carouse in the bars and taverns of Vila-Vila, of which there were not a few, and, soon enough, brawls would break out, thefts would occur, and Vila-Vila's reputation would drop another few notches.

However, the permanent residents of Vila-Vila were not entirely to blame. One could argue that, living in "houses" such as they had, there certainly existed no incentive to invest their earnings in goods that would only too soon be robbed, and there were surely no improvements to be made to their "homes" short of building new, durable ones—something very few of the families could afford to do.

Thus, Habitat's contribution to the growth and stability of Vila-Vila has been tremendous. Initially, thirty-three families were enrolled in the project, and work on their houses began. These houses would be constructed of concrete block, manufactured on site in Vila-Vila, with roofs of a fiber-cement material, cement floors, and doors and window-frames of wood, with an area of fifty-two square meters.

Sadly, due to a lack of sufficient prior education in Vila-Vila as to what Habitat was all about, there existed many rumors and speculations, most of them negative. The most common rumor was that Habitat represented a bank which, once a house was finished, would tack on a high interest rate. It was believed that then the family would be unable to pay and Habitat would end up with the family's lot and house. So, from the beginning, the Habitat representatives had their work cut out for them; not just seeing that the houses were built, but also working to demonstrate the truth about Habitat. . . .

Never Be the Same

Another thing that every International Partner writes about is how the experience changes his or her life. As Mark and Margee Frey (who served in Kinshasa, Zaire) wrote from Indianapolis, Indiana, after their return:

> It is said that once you have lived overseas, you will never be the same again. That is true for us. We can't go to Kroger and not be reminded of our hungry neighbors. We can't visit the malls and not see the rags the children wear every day. God has changed us. There is a huge chasm that separates us from those in need. In the early 1980s, Bill Moyers interviewed southern activist Miles Horton at the Highlander Center in Tennessee. At the end of the interview, Bill asked Miles what the big issue would be for the 1980s. Miles thoughtfully responded that the crisis between the haves and the have-nots would be the big issue and that it would be very painful because we all have family and friends on both sides. As Christians, we do have brothers and sisters on both sides. And we have all been changed in Christ so that we will not grow weary, but will work with all strength and speed in filling the great chasm that separates us. . . .

A Sacrifice?

And as for the sacrifices International Partners make, we'll let Mark and Gai Case, who served in the Philippines, sum up that thought, as well as this chapter, with words anyone will understand:

> We are privileged to be in Manila. That is important to say because many people think of what we are

doing as a sacrifice, something that must be very hard to do, something they could never do. Those thoughts could not be further from the truth. All we are trying to do is to give up our own agenda and to take on God's (Luke 9:23, 24). And who would be so brash as to say his own plans are better than his Creator's? It is hardly a sacrifice. And is it a difficult thing to do? No, the hard thing would be to ignore God's call to serve Him. Finally, the Lord's call to His own is not exclusive; this is something you could do if it is God's plan for you.

For information concerning how to become a Habitat for Humanity International Partner, write to International Partner Recruiter, Personnel Department, Habitat for Humanity International, Americus, Georgia 31709–3498.

Tallahassee, Florida, City Commissioner Jack McLean installs siding on Betty Brown's new Habitat house.

Ellie Pawelkop, along with husband Ozzie, from Tampa, Florida, volunteers in Americus (Ray Scioscia photos).

Volunteer Bill Bates takes count of large in-kind donation of lumber which he solicited.

President George Bush presents Volunteer Service Award to Amy Parsons who along with Rick Hathaway, was chosen to represent all Habitat volunteers at award ceremony at the White House (White House Press Corps photo).

Alan Derrick raises money for North Alabama HFH by "sign-sitting" for a week (Huntsville Times photo).

Timber framers blitz-build two Habitat houses in Hanover, Pennsylvania (Fine Homebuilding Magazine photo).

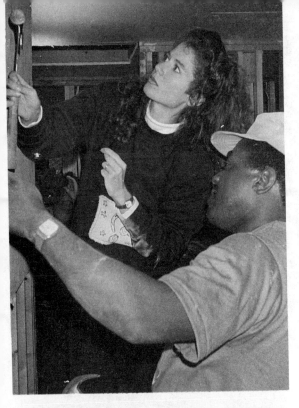

Christian Rock Singer Amy Grant works with Birmingham, Alabama, homeowner, Roosevelt Gordon, putting up sheetrock in his new home (November 1988). That evening she appeared in concert before 10,000 people at the Civic Center *(Birmingham Post-Herald* photo).

Dr. James Ferguson, founder of Habitat for Humanity in Papua New Guinea, preaches at house dedication in capital city of Port Moresby (Vera Randall photo, Sydney, Australia).

International Partners at work
. . . (above) loading fill dirt in
Peru and (below) mixing
mortar in Nicaragua.

II

Building Excitement in New Directions

8

Homeless Humanity/Disabled Humanity

During one afternoon of the 1988 Walk from Portland, Maine, to Atlanta, while waiting for the Boston rally to begin, we were walking around the area when we saw a cross erected in front of City Hall. Beside it was a conglomeration of cots with people on them. This "sleep-in" protest had been going on for several months, sponsored by an organization called Home Front '88. They were protesting the deaths of eighty-five homeless people in Boston the previous winter.

One of the people in that group was Bill Bates, a twenty-eight-year-old man who had been a homeless wanderer since he was eighteen. He had spent the last decade hitchhiking across all forty-eight contiguous states. Bill started talking to our people and decided he wanted to pick up his bedroll and come with us. He ended up walking all the way to Atlanta and then coming on to Americus to become a full-time volunteer. Bill is a very intelligent person. And he continues to be a valuable asset in our "in-kind" department, soliciting donated materials for Habitat projects all over the country.

A couple of days into the walk, Bill began talking about why he was homeless. "It all started back in '78 in Florida where I was born and raised," he said. "My dad and I had an argument and he threw me out of the house. So I hit the road and I've been somewhat in the transient state since then. I've been working here and there, but once you're transient, you go into a town and try to seek employment without an address and a home and it is awful hard to get good employment, good enough to sustain a house.

"Since April I've been working with the Home Front group, which is made up of homeless people and their supporters in the Boston area protesting the lack of affordable housing. We've been spending twenty-four hours a day at City Hall camping out and the whole time I've been there I've been wishing that we could do more than just sleep around. I see Habitat as an opportunity to do more."

Visible and Invisible

Bill now has a home with Habitat. But until that day he was one of approximately three million homeless persons in the United States,[1] a number that's steadily growing year by year. That's such a staggering number it's difficult to grasp the reality of it. Yet all of us can see these people in the streets, on the park benches, lying on the grates. We see them on the evening news and read about them in the newspapers.

The people on the streets are the visible homeless like Bill. But all the homeless people are not out on the streets for everyone to see. These others are the invisible ones. It is important to understand the difference.

There are fourteen million more people in the United States estimated to be "living on the knife edge of homelessness"—one paycheck away from being on the street.[2] That many more are in housing not fit for human habitation, but it is all they can afford. Some homeless people haven't missed a paycheck—but they're on the street anyway.

Tragically, many people have to choose between feeding themselves or having a place to stay. Obviously, people will choose to eat even if they have to live in their cars, double up with somebody, or even live outdoors. And the rest live in substandard housing since anything else is priced too high. Plus, their ranks are growing because additional apartments and houses are being vacated as a result of escalating rents. Housing costs, including rent and payments on mortgages, have increased to such a degree over the past ten years that only the affluent and a lesser number of middle class can afford to buy or rent a place to live. This has caused a crisis of the first magnitude. The ironic thing about the situation is that America has surplus housing—millions of vacant houses and apartments—but the Harvard Joint Center for Housing Studies estimates that 90 percent of these empty houses and apartments are at the top end of the market.

A father of four children recently told us, "Used to, I could find a place for $175 a month, but now it's more like $600 and my pay ain't gone up!"

Millard was in Boston a couple years ago participating in a dedication service for three new Habitat houses—one for a family that had been living with friends, their children sleeping in closets. The ones without friends are the ones who are the homeless.

Fallen through the Safety Nets

In December 1989, Raymond L. Flynn, Mayor of Boston, released a survey of twenty-seven cities by the U.S. Conference of Mayors which reported that their cities had so many requests from the homeless for help that they had to turn away families and others seeking shelter. And the percentage is rising steadily. These folks have fallen through all of the safety nets of our society and they have landed at the very bottom—homeless and hopeless and desperate.

The invisible homeless are not yet in the streets, but they could be on a day's notice. Living with friends or extended families in substandard houses, deteriorating tenements, or overcrowded apartments, some are better off than others, but all lack one or more of the basic necessities which make for adequate shelter. "One paycheck missed, one domestic argument, one major illness, or some major repair bill, and they are on the streets," says an American Affordable Housing Institute report. Once in the streets, the return trip is difficult if not nearly impossible without some assistance. Although the homeless have multiple needs, a roof is the common denominator, the one essential.

In the United States, we talk about the American dream of buying a home. Has it now become "the impossible dream" for many? What about the need of affordable housing in other countries?

Invisible Overseas

The largest segment of the "invisible" homeless are those outside the United States and Canada. The United Nations reports that between 1 and 1.5 billion people in the world live in substandard housing with 100 million of them lacking any shelter at all. In many cities of the developing nations, half of the people live in slum and squatter settlements. In some cities, more than three-fourths of the population live in such conditions. These people are invisible to most North Americans, but their pain is real and they are equally precious in God's sight.

No Starvation

Unlike many countries, the United States already has a policy of no starvation. There are food stamps, soup kitchens to feed the homeless, "meals on wheels" for the elderly. . . . Even prisoners are fed. Certainly, these programs need to continue. But Habitat for Humanity is making shelter a matter of conscience, too. We want the need for shelter to be dealt with just as seriously as hunger. And through the consciousness-raising efforts of Habitat for Humanity as well as the commitment media and other organizations have made toward this end, it is happening.

Habitat for the Homeless

Habitat for Humanity International's primary focus is on the "invisible" homeless, those living in substandard housing in North America and abroad. However, in mid-December 1988, the International Board of Directors voted unanimously to establish a new dimension to the work.

It's called Habitat for Homeless Humanity and it is now a program of Habitat for Humanity International. Our hearts are broken by the spectacle of so many men, women, boys, and girls wandering our streets, eating out of garbage cans and sleeping on grates and in front of doorways. We in Habitat for Humanity feel compelled to do something and this is our answer.

Some Habitat affiliates were already building and renovating houses for homeless people. In New York City, when the Habitat project renovated a building for nineteen needy families, one of the apartments was allotted to a man who had been living in a box behind the building. Also in New York City, Habitat made sleeping bags available to "street people" for a small charge.

In Atlanta, one of the twenty houses built by the Jimmy Carter Work Project in the summer of 1988 was for a man and three children who moved into their new home from a shelter. He had a job but couldn't afford any housing because his income was so low. A project in North Carolina built a house for a family that was living in an abandoned bus. The Habitat project in Cartersville, Georgia, built a house for a family that had been staying in a storage shed. The new Habitat project in Hawaii selected a homeless family living in a fire station.

Sometimes Habitat works with other groups to provide shelter for homeless people. In 1988, the mayor of Charleston, South Carolina, Joseph Riley, responded to a growing homeless population by creating the Mayor's Task Force on Homelessness. Groups as disparate as the Salvation Army, the Chamber of Commerce, the Veterans Administration, and the Charleston Police Department banded together to bring their various backgrounds to bear on easing the burdens carried by those who have no homes. One idea suggested was to build some small, one-bedroom houses for men coming out of a local shelter. An architect volunteered his services, and soon plans were unveiled for 264-square-foot, heated homes modeled after the Freedman's Cottages built in Charleston for former slaves following the Civil War. It soon became obvious that a Habitat-shaped vacuum was being created. So members of Sea Island Habitat for Humanity in nearby Johns Island helped to set up a new affiliate called Charleston Habitat for Humanity that would "partner" with the other members of the Task Force and organize the actual construction of the houses.

The idea is just taking the concept of Habitat for Humanity

one step further. What we're suggesting to affiliates in areas with a homeless problem is to set up a division to help homeless people by providing transitional housing. Gwinnett County Habitat for Humanity, north of Atlanta, was the first Habitat affiliate to officially add a "homeless" division to its regular building program. On May 24, 1989, we were at the dedication of a home already giving temporary shelter and assistance to two homeless families with room for an additional three families. Linda led the prayer of dedication for the historic first Habitat for Homeless Humanity program. (Unfortunately, neighbors objected to this facility and it eventually closed, but the local group expects to reopen another house in a nearby area.)

Since that beginning of Habitat for Homeless Humanity, many studies and articles appearing in newspapers and magazines have confirmed that the program is on the right track. For instance, an article titled, "American Survey" in the May 1989 issue of *The Economist* magazine states, ". . . the shock of homelessness destroys a person's self-confidence. And the cards may already have been stacked against him [her/them]. Surveys show that most homeless people face multiple obstacles: they may be poorly educated, drink too much, take drugs, have been in prison. They need a bridge back to self-sufficiency. One of these bridges is 'transitional' housing: small super-shelters where a homeless person is helped to draw breath for a few months before moving on to a permanent home."

Super-Shelters with a Twist

These "super-shelters" are just what Habitat for Humanity has in mind—but with a twist.

The shelter will be a very special kind of place, one for people who are capable of home ownership or who can be trained to become homeowners. It will enable Habitat to go lower on the economic scale and get some people eventually into houses who otherwise might never be able to make it. These transition shelters will be places where homeless individuals and families can come in off the streets and have a decent living situation until a more permanent habitation can be built or renovated for them.

Are these shelters for all homeless people? The answer is a clear "No," because some homeless people are not capable of home ownership.

Shelters for such people are needed, of course, but our unique calling is to provide housing for people who are capable of home ownership. We realize that this ministry cannot do everything. We must stick to our calling. But we do feel that Habitat can make a difference in this one area of homelessness and do it quite naturally as a logical extension of the work.

Help Them Back to Wholeness

Many people are now living in the streets who are, or can be, prepared for home ownership. How will we go about helping them? First, homeless people can be housed in a shelter. If possible, they will pay some amount of rent during their stay. Second, when feasible, they will be involved in finding solutions to their problems and opportunities will be provided to take on leadership roles. Homeless people may be without a place to live, but many possess untapped talent, creativity, knowledge, and skills. We certainly have seen that in Bill Bates. As one formerly homeless woman put it, "Homeless people are homeless, not necessarily helpless."

Our workers will help develop job skills, counsel about personal problems, and love people back to wholeness. Finally, when the time is right, folks in transitional Habitat housing can apply, like any other family, for a regular Habitat house. They will do their sweat equity in building or renovating their new house, and, when finished, move in and pay for it, month by month, just like any other Habitat partner family.

Starting Off Small

The idea is for Habitat projects to start off small by renovating or building a house and making it available for two or three homeless individuals or families. Then they work with the people to prepare them for home ownership. One such house was completed by Spokane Habitat for Humanity and occupied in the spring of 1990 by two homeless families.[3] Other transitional houses are being planned by the Dallas, Texas, and Columbus, Georgia, Habitat affiliates.

This concept is not for the faint-hearted. There will be difficulties. Many homeless people have problems beyond available resources. They have gotten their lives jangled, jumbled, torn up, and, in many cases, almost destroyed. It will take a lot of patience and grace to work with them. But so many are like Bill. All they need is a chance.

Habitat for Humanity with Disabilities

Another exciting development is Habitat for Humanity with Disabilities. This concern for the physically disabled began as a "special affiliate" in 1984 under the leadership of Joe and Stephanie Thomas in Milledgeville, Georgia. It was moved to International headquarters in the summer of 1988.

This program gives technical and financial assistance to Habitat projects that are building or renovating homes for persons with disabilities. It also serves to encourage the building of barrier-free housing and to teach how to build such housing.

Advocacy groups such as Concrete Change, based in Atlanta, and Joni & Friends, a Christian ministry to persons with disabilities that is headquartered in Agoura Hills, California, have been very helpful. Joni Eareckson Tada, founder and president of Joni & Friends, herself a quadriplegic, spoke eloquently at the Twelfth Anniversary Celebration in Atlanta. She urged that all homes be built for barrier-free accessibility. She explained, "Even though a house is not occupied by a disabled person, it should be barrier-free to accommodate disabled visitors." Her point was well taken.

Since the Celebration, Joni and her husband Ken have generously given of their time and knowledge to meet with Habitat staff and others within the Habitat organization who have accessibility as a special interest.

Habitat for Humanity with Disabilities has set a goal that all Habitat homes be constructed for barrier-free accessibility. This helps persons with mobility impairments who may visit and prevents the need for major structural changes if the homeowner becomes disabled.

Patty Hayes, a barrier-free design consultant in Milwaukee, learned about Habitat for Humanity from hearing talk about a Jimmy Carter Work Project. One of the six houses to be built during the project would be for a person with disabilities. So she called us to offer assistance in planning the house. She helped with the design of house number four in the 1989 Carter Work Project. A disabled couple, both of whom use wheelchairs, are now happily occupying the house.

Using a wheelchair herself, Patty had discovered (sometimes the hard way) that a person with physical disabilities had more needs than just an access ramp and wide doorways. She shared some minor innovations in her own apartment that made a world of difference—like taking out carpet; removing thresholds and door jambs to make the best surface for easy mobility; installing sliding doors for bathrooms, bedrooms, and closets; eliminating all unnecessary doors; and mounting sinks and stoves at table-top height.

These kinds of changes can run into some money, but Patty told how she was able to keep costs down by smart use of standard products. Better still, Patty suggested, it is easy and cost-effective to make changes with a pencil and eraser at the blueprint stage.

The previous year, at the 1988 Jimmy Carter Work Project in Atlanta, two of the twenty houses built were specially equipped for wheelchair accessibility.

Some exciting steps have already been taken toward the goal of barrier-free housing. Suggested building criteria for affiliates now include wider doors and halls and at least one no-step entrance with sloped walkway, where possible. In Americus, it has been decided that all Habitat homes built from now on will have some additional features, including lowered light switches, raised electrical outlets, and wood backing around tubs and toilets for easy installation of grab bars if needed in the future.

Importance of an Adequate House

The story of Richard Hayes dramatically illustrates the importance of an adequate house for a disabled person. Richard is a quadriplegic who was injured in a semi-trailer truck accident.

He had no insurance, and draws only a small check from Social Security. His wife works in a nursing home for minimum wages. With two young children, they lived in a small apartment. Richard couldn't get his wheelchair into the bedroom, kitchen, or bathroom without his wife's help.

Their Habitat house in Oklahoma City has ramps, wide doors, and a shower he can roll his chair into. There is a swing set, sandbox, and a garden spot in the fenced back yard for the children.

Richard said, "The foundation had to be dug out from under this house, the house jacked up and another foundation poured. Those men worked in all kinds of bad weather and I never heard a single complaint. Every one of them could have been doing something better, but they just wanted to help people. That's the kind of Christians they are. There were some young Methodist kids here scraping off old paint on the outside of the house. It started raining and they just kept working. They weren't getting paid. They were just feeling good about helping someone.

"I saw former President and Mrs. Carter on TV talking about Habitat and working on a house up in Milwaukee. It is amazing to me that a former president and first lady would do what these folks here are doing for me. I have really seen what Christians are all about. It's just remarkable that young kids and retired people, men and women, bankers and builders, all of different denominations, are working together to help someone that they never knew before.

"I just have one regret. I can't help them out. They say 'Would someone hand me a hammer?' And my hands won't pick up a hammer. But I can do one thing. I have a special telephone that I can hit with my knuckles and dial, and I have a good strong voice. I can call the volunteers when another crew is needed. That will help some. Then I can tell people about my enthusiasm for Habitat."

Wheelies

When we visited Port Moresby, Papua New Guinea, in March 1988, we participated in the dedication of two houses built for what they termed "Wheelies"—persons who use wheelchairs. It was such a joy to meet these people and see how happy they were with their new houses. One family of "Wheelies" had been living in cramped hospital quarters, unable to find suitable housing because most traditional houses in that country are built on stilts.

As more and more people learn of Habitat for Humanity, we in the Americus headquarters are contacted on almost a daily basis about all kinds of special housing needs. For example, there have been requests for Habitat to build more houses for the elderly, housing for people with Hansen's Disease (leprosy), and chemical-free housing for people suffering from environmental illnesses. The list goes on and on.

Another Special Outreach—Hope House

More and more, we learn of these unique needs. Happily, quite a few Habitat projects are already addressing some of their own areas' special needs—or they will be in the future. For example, in Savannah, Georgia, Coastal Empire Habitat for Humanity renovated an old abandoned house and sold it at no profit and no interest to another nonprofit group, Hope House for Savannah, Inc., which now operates "Hope House" for unwed pregnant young women.

Special Habitat for special people. The aim is to help, and, as the ministry grows, to uncover all sorts of needs that Habitat's housing expertise can address. And we look forward to the wonderful difference each of these avenues of Habitat will make in people's lives.

9

Campus Chapters

It started with a phone call.

Gary Cook, director of denominational and community relations and assistant to the president at Baylor University, called to invite Millard to speak at chapel in November 1987.

Gary had known about Habitat for Humanity for some time and had a personal interest and involvement in the new Habitat affiliate in Waco, Texas.

But Gary had something else in mind. He had an idea. Why not have Habitat start chapters on college campuses? And why not have the first one be at Baylor University?

What an idea! We were immediately excited about the potential of the concept. If we could get college and university students all over the country and, eventually, in other countries, involved in raising money and awareness and even doing hands-on construction, the effect could be enormous on the whole movement of Habitat for Humanity.

Millard's trip to Baylor was a great success. More than 2,000 students attended chapel and they responded very positively to the challenge of starting the first campus chapter of Habitat for Humanity. Following his talk, there was an official commissioning of the campus chapter. Baylor student Ward Hayworth was named first chapter president. Baylor President Dr. Herbert Reynolds and several other faculty and staff became charter members along with 200 students. Soon the Baylor group was heavily involved in helping to build houses with the Waco affiliate and making plans to raise funds as well as organize work groups to go to other Habitat sites both in the United States and in Central America.

In the weeks ahead, we "fleshed out" the concept of campus chapters and named the first director, David Eastis, a dynamic young man from San Jose, California. David quickly organized a campus chapter department at headquarters in Americus and started getting out the word to colleges and universities. Fittingly, Gary Cook was named president of the Habitat for Humanity College and University Chapters Association.

Campus Chapter Goals

The concept of campus chapters was that college and university groups would be formed all across the land primarily to help local Habitat affiliates raise money and build houses. Each group would have a student president, but anyone on campus could join, including staff and faculty. Even a staff or faculty person would be encouraged to hold one of the offices, such as secretary or treasurer, to insure continuity of the group.

All money raised would be quickly turned over to the local Habitat affiliate or to Habitat for Humanity International. Only a small amount of funds would be retained by the chapter for administrative expenses. And no chapter would build or renovate houses except in cooperation with a Habitat project.

The chapters would seek to recruit volunteers for their work with local affiliates (for Saturdays, evenings, holidays, or spring break), or for a work camp which would go to some distant location in North America or overseas for a week or two. They'd also seek to recruit students to work full-time with Habitat following graduation, either in the United States or abroad, as well as encourage students to remain involved with Habitat as part-time volunteers after college by joining the local effort in the city they move to. And where there was not an affiliate, it is hoped, they would help start one.

The goal on every campus where a chapter was formed would be to make Habitat for Humanity a "household word." And the official motto of campus chapters would be, "Love should not be just words and talk; it must be true love, which shows itself in action" (1 John 3:18, TEV).

And with those ideals in mind, we were ready to begin.

Some Colleges Ahead of Us

The association had but one member, Baylor University, even though several colleges and universities were already helping local affiliates and overseas sponsored projects in significant ways. They had simply not established a formal Habitat organization on campus.

Back in 1984, Jim Lundeen, an administrator at Chicago's North Park College, rallied a group of students to "adopt" a house and family in the Habitat project in the Westside neighborhood of the city.

Over the next four years, North Park's Habitat outreach not only completed that first house, they also helped build or renovate several others. In June 1988, the group officially became a campus chapter. By late 1989, the chapter had worked on a total of sixteen houses in Chicago, and had helped start two more Habitat affiliates in the city (Uptown and Albany Park). In addition, North Park graduates, along with leaders of their "Make-A-Difference" summer camp program, have been instrumental in starting five new Habitat affiliates across the country.

Four other college groups also predated the campus chapter program. Students at Eastern College in St. Davids, Pennsylvania, Western Michigan University in Kalamazoo, Wheaton College in Wheaton, Illinois, and DePauw University in Greencastle, Indiana, had already caught "Infectious Habititis" and were doing great things.

Habitat board member Tony Campolo had fired up the students at Eastern about Habitat for Humanity. For a couple of years before the chapters program began they had been going out in groups helping to build houses in the nearby affiliates in Philadelphia. Several Eastern graduates entered the International Partner program to work overseas with Habitat.

Western Michigan University students had been regularly helping out at the Kalamazoo Habitat affiliate for a couple of years prior to their becoming an official campus chapter in September 1988. Students at Wheaton College had raised over $40,000 and spent their spring break renovating a building with two apartments for the Westside Habitat project in Chicago.

And under the leadership of Chaplain Fred Lamar, students

at DePauw University had been sending out students to work at Habitat projects since 1983. The work with Habitat was part of a larger program at DePauw which sent groups of students all over the world during their January term to do hands-on mission work. The program is so successful that other universities regularly come to DePauw to study how it operates.

These highly motivated DePauw students have worked in Habitat projects in Peru, Guatemala, Mexico, Immokalee, Florida, and Americus, Georgia. In early 1990, the school formed an official campus chapter to work with the new Habitat affiliate in Greencastle. Our youngest daughter, Georgia, then a freshman at DePauw, was an enthusiastic charter member.

Second Chapter

The second official campus chapter was formed at the College of Wooster in Wooster, Ohio. It was approved on March 6, 1988. The new group went straight to work. The chapter's first president, Chris Alghini, arranged to have a Habitat for Humanity house on campus where several chapter members could live. In the first year of their organizational life, the College of Wooster chapter often sent work groups to the local Wayne County affiliate and to the nearby Akron affiliate.

Then they learned that the university planned to demolish five houses on campus to make room for another college building. So Chris talked the university into donating the houses to Wayne County Habitat and then he and the other chapter members helped the local affiliate raise over $100,000 to move and renovate the houses for low-income families. They also helped start a campus chapter at Malone College in Canton, Ohio.

The Good Word Spreads

Throughout the spring and summer of 1988, word spread far and wide about the new campus chapters program. Millard talked about campus chapters in practically every speech he made and in every letter he wrote. We wanted to have at least ten official chapters formed by the time of the big Twelfth Anniversary Celebration in Atlanta in September. Amazingly, by early September, there were not ten chapters, but twenty-six!

Applications by Overnight Mail

Colleges began to send their applications by overnight mail to our headquarters. By the time the Celebration started in Atlanta on Thursday, September 15, a total of thirty-four applications had been received. Then, the next day, two more applications arrived from East Texas State University and the University of Akron. A total of thirty-six chapters would receive their charter later that evening.

Why Not High Schools?

During the following month, two more milestones were reached. On October 8, Marist School, a Roman Catholic day school in Atlanta for young men and women attending grades seven through twelve, became the first high school to form a campus chapter of Habitat for Humanity. It was the thirty-eighth chapter.

Martin Brooks, a young man from Vestal, New York, joined the campus chapters department in Americus to direct the high school campus chapters program.

Over the next few months, four more high schools followed Marist in organizing official campus chapters: Jesuit High School in Tampa, Florida; Mount Greylock Regional High School in Williamstown, Massachusetts; Northern High School in Durham, North Carolina; and Hotchkiss School in Lakeville, Connecticut. (In April 1989, Martin left Americus to start his college career at Cornell University. He promptly formed a campus chapter there.)

And Why Not Seminaries?

The second milestone which occurred in October 1988 was the acceptance of the first chapter at a seminary. Actually, the chapter is at a college and seminary—Bethel College and Seminary in St. Paul, Minnesota. This new organization began with 130 members. Four months later, in February 1989, Asbury Theological Seminary in Wilmore, Kentucky, became the second seminary with a campus chapter.

By mid-1989, we had put this "little idea" on a sound footing and acquired a new director, David McDaniels, the Protestant chaplain at Ithaca College as well as organizer of that school's campus chapter. Seventy chapters had been approved in twenty-five states and the District of Columbia. Reports from the chapters revealed that 3,700 volunteers had raised over $277,000 and had put in more than 18,000 hours in building and renovating houses at Habitat project sites. Several of these student volunteers had come to work in the campus chapters department in Americus, and a Campus Chapters Advisory Council had been organized to help give guidance to the evolving Habitat chapters movement.

As of this writing, there are more than 100 chapters scattered all across the United States and they are raising tens of thousands of dollars and putting in thousands of hours at various Habitat work sites.[1]

Creative Fund-Raisers

Students are creative fund-raisers. They have devised many ingenious ways to generate funds and promote awareness of Habitat's work. Calvin College in Grand Rapids, Michigan, organized a "Bike to Build" race which raised over $22,000. The University of Richmond organized two bike races which generated nearly $40,000. The University of Akron chapter held a boat race, "Row for Dough," which produced $1,400. Whitworth College in Spokane, Washington invented a "Moronathon" that resulted in $800. (A "moronathon" is a wacky kind of marathon. The students received pledges to walk half a mile, run three-fourths of a mile, and swim one lap in the campus pool. To add to the fun, some tied themselves together with rope, crawled, and did somersaults.) Marist School had a volleyball tournament which made $1,000. Stacey Steck of American University in the nation's capital also put on a volleyball event called "Spike for Humanity." It brought in $700. Ithaca College did a ten-mile relay called "Run for Love." And the College of Wooster organized a "Rocking Chair-A-Thon."

But the chapters have done so much more than raise money and furnish workers. The chapter at Auburn University, for instance, was instrumental in forming a local Habitat affiliate in their county in east Alabama.

The Duke University chapter in Durham, North Carolina, is one of the most active and successful chapters in the country. This dynamic group conducted a very effective teaching and consciousness-raising activity in November 1988 called "Link Together to Break the Chains of Hunger and Homelessness." And the chapter has sent work teams to West Virginia, south Florida, New York City, and to several affiliates in North Carolina.

The chapter at Rhodes College in Memphis, Tennessee, raised enough money to build an entire house with the local affiliate—Mid-South Habitat for Humanity—and then the students went out and built it!

The chapter at Ball State University in Muncie, Indiana, built on campus the component parts for a house and then transported them to Sumter, South Carolina, where the house was assembled for a Habitat family.

The Future

In the years ahead, we have no doubt that these campus chapters will increasingly become a truly awesome force in the overall movement of Habitat for Humanity. Duke University Campus Chapter President Sally Higgins, explains quite eloquently why the chapters are meaningful to students: "School offers more than just preparation; it can also be a time for action. Campus chapters of Habitat for Humanity provide students with the opportunities to put their love into action. And students increasingly are proving that they are idealistic enough to dream, compassionate enough to care, and responsible enough to act."

Within his first few weeks as director of campus chapters, David McDaniels came up with an exciting idea: The "Coahoma Collegiate Challenge: Spring Break Building Blitz; Six Houses in Six Weeks."

What is the challenge? Habitat for Humanity has pledged to eliminate poverty housing in Coahoma, Mississippi, in five years. (The Christian organization World Vision is a partner with Habitat in this challenge.) Coahoma is a small delta town which has only about 350 people, around sixty families. Almost all housing is substandard. The average annual family income is $4,100, so house payments cannot exceed $100 a month. Campus chapters contributed by raising $60,000, enough to build six houses in Coahoma. An additional $6,000 was raised to build six more houses overseas. Students from twenty-six campus chapters were recruited to build the Coahoma houses in early 1990 with one house being dedicated each Friday over the six-week period.

God is truly blessing the work of campus chapters. They are a magnificent extension of the ministry of Habitat for Humanity. Already the chapters program is connecting young people and adults on campuses around the United States with both local and foreign Habitat projects.

Gary Cook, now president of Dallas Baptist University, first surmised that we could look forward to seeing 300 to 400 chapters in ten years. Instead we are convinced that we'll have that many in half the time and they will not only be in the United States, but also in Canada, Australia, and many other countries. So, the excitement is building on campuses, and it is building fast and furious. We couldn't be more pleased about this new Habitat direction.

10

Covenant Churches

"Churches have been our backbone," says Rick Beech, executive director of Habitat for Humanity of Wake County, North Carolina.

And so it should be.

When Jimmy Carter speaks about Habitat, he often reminds audiences that if churches and synagogues would commit to build at least one or two houses every year, the problem of poverty housing could be delivered a knockout blow. You see, there are nearly 350,000 churches and synagogues in the United States and another 30,000 in Canada.[1]

And that very real potential is the driving force behind Habitat's new covenant church program.

Even though the program is relatively new, hundreds of churches are already Habitat for Humanity covenant churches. They are made up of all denominations, races, and cultural backgrounds, but they have at least one thing in common. They believe in the idea of building decent homes for and with needy families as an expression of their faith.

"The Church That Helps People"

On the 700-mile Walk from Americus to Indianapolis in 1983, we stopped in Cartersville, Georgia, and were hosted by the town's Episcopal church. We found that congregation to be a very loving and concerned one that did a lot of outreach to the surrounding community. At that particular time they were giving out electric fans in the summer to people who were too poor to have air conditioning as well as feeding hungry people and helping transients who came through town.

While we were there, one of the members told us about the time someone called another church in town and asked, "Is this the church that helps people?" The secretary replied, "No, that's not our church. It's the one on Cherokee Avenue."

That kind of response evokes a little laughter but it's also sad, isn't it? Thank God, some churches do just want to help people. They strive to live by Matthew 25, taking to heart its practical list of how Christians can incarnate the Good News with food, clothing, water, and shelter. They work with the basics of life as part of their ministry, and people never fail to notice.

Save the Lost and Build Houses?

No one can argue that a significant portion of the church's mission is to teach the Word and save the lost. Many churches, unfortunately, fail to see that their mission should go any further.

A man confided to Millard that he was "downright tired of getting saved. Every Sunday," he said, "the pastor preaches, 'Get saved. Get saved.' He never goes beyond that."

After hearing about Habitat for Humanity, though, he was excited about getting himself and his church involved with some sort of practical application of the Word. We hear this often—church members who are ready to "do something" along with "talking."

And Habitat is one more way to do God's work. Rather than take away from existing programs in the church, covenant churches have found that Habitat actually enhances those ministries. Adult groups enjoy a new type of fellowship and camaraderie when they work together at a construction site. Young people learn about God's love through practical Habitat experiences. Churches, raising money for Habitat, are pleasantly surprised to find that their overall mission giving increases.

How Does It Work?

Covenant churches, in an annually renewable written commitment—a commitment of faith—pledge to pray for Habitat's ministry and to contribute financially in some way. Beyond that,

131

each church defines its own commitment based on its particular needs and interests. In turn, Habitat for Humanity presents each church with a covenant church certificate (suitable for framing), supplies literature, arranges for a Habitat representative to attend the church and answer questions, and provides opportunities to serve in ways the congregation feels comfortable with. Habitat also promises to carefully manage the money, volunteers, time, and other donated resources.

The covenant churches are encouraged to work with Habitat in as many of the following ways as possible:

- Spread the word about Habitat for Humanity's worldwide ministry throughout the community.

- Organize work parties to help build houses with a local affiliate.

- Select a church member to be actively involved on the board of directors or a committee of a local affiliate.

- Provide office space and/or office assistance for the local affiliate.

- Support "Vision Habitat" by collecting eyeglasses. (This program at Habitat's international headquarters collects old eyeglasses and ships them overseas to be sold at minimal cost. Funds raised are used to build houses.)[2]

- Hold an Alternative Christmas Market offering church members the opportunity to "purchase" construction supplies to build houses as alternatives to traditional holiday gift-giving.

- Distribute Habitat "house banks" and devotional guides to church members.

- Promote Habitat projects abroad by inviting Habitat for Humanity staff, board members, and International Partners to speak in the church and community.

- Celebrate the International Day of Prayer and Action for Human Habitat annually on the third Sunday of September.

(The International Day of Prayer and Action for Human Habitat is a way churches can join together on a particular day to make shelter a matter of conscience for the world. Thousands of churches, including Habitat's Covenant Churches, observe this special Sunday by making shelter concerns a part of worship services. The use of shelter-related scriptures, responsive readings, prayers, sermons, and music is all directed toward understanding the problem and evoking action for decent housing for those in need. Materials are available from Habitat headquarters to assist churches with their observance of International Day of Prayer and Action for Human Habitat.)

Churches Have Always Been There

When the forerunner of this unique partnership housing program began at Koinonia Farm in the late sixties, scores of churches lent all kinds of support—letters of affirmation to Koinonia with a commitment to pray for the ministry, checks sent monthly or annually to the Fund for Humanity, or orders for large quantities of Koinonia's pecan products sold to finance the house-building efforts. Some of these same churches began supporting our house-building efforts overseas when we moved to Zaire in 1973.[3]

Even back then, the Plymouth Congregational Church in Plymouth, New Hampshire, started giving $2,000 annually—enough to build at least one house a year for a poor family in Zaire. And they are still doing it.

The Beginning of Covenant Churches

So the covenant church idea, the formal "partnership" between Habitat and local churches, was natural. This idea began in the Habitat Northeast Regional Center as a means of officially engaging churches in assisting with Habitat development. Finding it so successful in the Northeast, Habitat International adopted the covenant church program in 1987 as a viable way to give recognition and assistance to churches already actively supporting Habitat for Humanity and as an effective means of recruiting more churches in the effort.[4]

We have many exciting stories of how churches are helping in the growing work of Habitat for Humanity.

Change Someone's Life

Germantown United Methodist Church in Rossville near Memphis, Tennessee, led the construction of Mattie Winton's house and had it ready for the family to occupy in early 1989. Over 200 families from that church joined a "Change Someone's Life With Your Change" campaign to raise $28,000. More than 100 people gave 2,500 hours of labor during the last five months of 1988. Forty families provided lunch for the workers each Saturday. These people were looking for a way to glorify Jesus with their service, and they succeeded.

Size Makes No Difference

A church's size makes no difference in enthusiastic support. Triumph the Church and Kingdom of God in Christ in Melbourne, Florida, is a church of sixty members. Instead of pledging a budgeted amount, the church collects an offering every three months for Habitat's work. Most church members attend house dedications and many volunteer in house construction.

A church of 700 members, Colonial Heights Presbyterian in Kingsport, Tennessee, took on the challenge to build an entire house. This meant raising $25,000 and providing 100 volunteer worker days. They called it their "Five-Day Miracle House." Through pledges from church members, church suppers, and recycling cans and newspapers, this church ended up raising $30,000.

When the house was finished, Pastor David Wadsworth exclaimed, "This house-raising was the single most inspiring project I have yet been part of in my eleven years as a pastor. The spirit of cooperation and sense of community surrounding Habitat work is amazing."

One church member stated, "I have never felt closer to God

than when we were working on the 'Five-Day Miracle House.'"
And before work was complete on that first house, members
started asking, "When are we going to build another one?"

Your Church Is Going to Build a House

Bryan Stamper, pastor of St. Paul's Presbyterian Church in
Orlando, Florida, had a vision in which God said to him, "Your
church is going to build a house." Then he read an article about
Colonial Heights Presbyterian's "Five-Day Miracle House"
in an issue of our *Habitat World* newspaper and shared it with
his congregation. The members got all excited about building
a home with a family in one of the poor neighborhoods of
Orlando, so they began making plans to work with the local
affiliate.

Pastor Stamper asked the president of the local Home
Builder's Association, Rick Dye, if he could help with contacts.
Rick became so enthusiastic that he volunteered to build the
whole house with the help of the local Home Builders Association. Naturally, after getting his church so pumped up, Pastor
Stamper was not willing for that to happen so the two groups
made plans to blitz-build the house together.

The people selected to receive the house were Jean and
David Brooks and their three little girls. Jean and David had
moved to Orlando two and a half years earlier seeking work and
had spent their first month at a local shelter for the homeless.

Originally scheduled to be completed in two weeks, the
house was blitz-built in ten days during the summer of 1989.

Afterward, Pastor Stamper described the benefits of such
an experience: "It enables people who have not yet had leadership roles in the church to become involved. And it breaks down
stereotypes of what less-fortunate people are like. Both the husband and wife in the family had jobs. They were diligent and
hard-working people who, with a little bit of love and care,
could make it on their own."

And here's the best part—the members of St. Paul's enjoyed their experience with Habitat so much that they set for
themselves a new goal, an entire subdivision of twenty Habitat
houses in the greater Orlando area.

Inspiring Each Other

In 1987, Edenton Street United Methodist Church became the first church in Raleigh, North Carolina, to build a Habitat house. Two years later, the local Habitat for Humanity group had eleven houses under way with seven of those being built in partnership with churches of various denominations.

The affiliate asked each church to contribute $33,000 cash and/or in-kind gifts plus nine Saturdays of labor. (Actually, the church members volunteered much more than expected as they became more and more excited about the project.) The affiliate also trained church members to be nurturers for Habitat home-owners and asked them to commit one year to work with a family on budgeting, home maintenance, and other needs as they arose.

A coalition of two black churches (Martin Street Baptist and Laodicea United Church of Christ) and two white churches (Pullen Memorial Baptist and Community United Church of Christ) built a house together.

At this same North Carolina affiliate, a 204-member church, Providence Holiness, became a covenant church committed to raising $33,000 and providing ten volunteer labor days. The pastor said: "This project is highly motivational for our members. We want more than just a God-talk; we want a God-walk."

Youth Take the Lead

Also in North Carolina, twenty-five tenth, eleventh, and twelfth graders from Charlotte's St. John Baptist Church spent a week in the summer of 1989 putting up a house. Previously, this young group had conducted vacation Bible schools for inner-city kids in places like New York and Chicago. But this year they wanted to do a mission project at home. So they attended training sessions on house construction and raised $32,500 by doing yard work and other odd jobs around town. The group stayed in the dormitory of a local college. Beginning work as early as 7:00 A.M., the students had virtually completed the house by week's end. All it lacked was a few finishing touches. Although young people have participated in Habitat projects across the country, this was the first time a youth crew had taken on building an entire house with limited adult supervision.

Sunday schoolers of Asbury United Methodist Church in Salisbury, Maryland, decided to help Habitat by collecting a mile of pennies. Estimating it would take 87,500 pennies, the children took Habitat "house banks" home with them and periodically brought what they collected to the church. After several months, they totaled up their pennies and presented them to a Habitat representative at a morning worship service. They had collected $1,176.69! It took two wheelbarrows to hold the bags of pennies as ushers brought them down the aisle making several trips. The children were so thrilled by the results they decided to continue collecting and giving to Habitat.

Churches Help in Many Ways

Biz Ostberg of Appalachia Habitat wrote us about a church in Oak Ridge, Tennessee, that organized a campaign termed "Miracle Sunday." During two services on one Sunday they collected in cash and pledges over $175,000 for mission projects. Besides funding a Habitat house, money was designated for a solar-powered generator at a hospital in Africa, a building for a day-care center in east Tennessee, and renovation of their own building to make it accessible for the physically disabled.

First Congregational Church of Kent, Connecticut, opened up the Quality Thrift Shop as a means of raising money for needs in their community as well as abroad. The thrift shop serving the town and surrounding areas supplies good clothes at low prices. The congregation chose to use some of the earnings to build Habitat houses in Assinman, Ghana ($1,500 each).

We've already reported on the tremendous commitment of money and people by Atlanta's Peachtree Presbyterian Church. Dr. Frank Harrington, pastor of the church, and the people of that fine congregation continue to inspire us all.

Australia's First Covenant Church

The covenant church idea is even spreading abroad. When Habitat was organized in Australia and was ready to find support through churches, Doug Allen was contacted. Doug, managing director of a computer services company in a Sydney suburb, had heard Tony Campolo speak to a group of Australian businessmen in 1988 and was inspired by the examples Tony gave of creative Christian ministry—one of them being Habitat for Humanity. Doug was intrigued and let it be known he was interested. And so when Habitat contacted him, he immediately organized a group from his church, Castle Hill Church of Christ, to meet with Habitat people. The church soon decided to become Australia's first covenant church, adopting five townhouse units planned in Sydney and committing to raising $10,000 in cash and $20,000 in donated materials in addition to supplying all kinds of volunteer labor. And since then, they've found even more creative ways to help Habitat Australia, including a big festival which raised over $5,000 in one day.

Adopt-a-Home

Milwaukee Habitat for Humanity has several churches that provide primary support, leadership, and volunteers for house building and rehab work through an "Adopt-a-Home" program.

St. Pius X Catholic Church was one of the first churches to work with the Milwaukee affiliate. Members used pledge cards during Habitat Awareness Month at the church to commit dollars, materials, or volunteer time for house building.

"Adopt-a-Home" programs are found at many Habitat affiliates all across the country. It is a plan whereby a church, group of churches, or others can take responsibility for building a Habitat house, including fund-raising, construction, and working with the family. Thus, loving relationships can develop within churches, among churches, with Habitat homeowners, and throughout the community as a whole.

A number of churches participate in an Adopt-a-Home program by providing volunteers to work on a house with people from another church. Usually, ten to a dozen new volunteers are "teamed" with a like number from a congregation with more experience. In that way, work groups are ecumenical, diverse, and sufficiently skilled to do quality building.

Sometimes the Adopt-a-Home program is exactly what an affiliate needs, especially in urban areas where so many factors are competing for people's time, talents, and resources. Jim Lundeen of Uptown Chicago Habitat wrote us that numbers really weren't the problem in getting things going with that new affiliate. Their mailing list consisted of 3,000 people. The problem was that those 3,000 didn't know each other. Like many affiliates in needy urban neighborhoods, those who were taking an active part on the affiliate board were overstressed neighborhood people along with a few scattered urbanites. The project was really bogged down, even though everyone wanted rapid progress.

Then Jim learned about Adopt-a-Home from Mid-South Habitat for Humanity, Memphis, Tennessee, and things began to happen. "North Park College, Northwest Covenant Church (a small suburban church), and Fourth Presbyterian (a large down-town church), as well as a suburban coalition of five churches— and even an individual—all have adopted homes and families," Jim said. "The individual, a builder, is already working on his second home!"

Among the groups working with Uptown, Jim noticed that Adopt-a-Home meant a commitment to see the whole project through, all the way through: "Adopt-a-Home means raising all the money for land and building in our heavily impacted and gentrifying Chicago neighborhood, chairing committees that work closely with affiliate leadership, finding donated materials, recruiting volunteers, and working closely with the selected family in partnership—to nurture them and support them, to build a house and a home."

Adopt-a-Home was just the focus and push that Uptown Habitat needed to get on its feet and running. And other churches and groups are learning about the Adopt-a-Home program and are coming forward to sign on to help build more houses.

Why Should a Church Build Houses?
Urban, rural, suburban, evangelical, liberal, conservative, or any other type of church you can think of can get involved in the ministry of Habitat for Humanity by becoming an official or unofficial covenant church or by being part of Adopt-a-Home.

But some people might wonder why churches should involve themselves in such down-to-earth activities. At first glance, Habitat for Humanity may appear to deal with only the physical aspects of providing shelter. However, with a closer look, one can see that Habitat deals with profound Christian teachings.

People sometimes ask us if Habitat for Humanity is evangelistic. We reply that it is very evangelistic because the ministry is seeking to write the Christian gospel on the hearts of people, and to write it in such a way that their lives are changed, so that they think about themselves and their neighbors in a different way and see their communities in a new light.

If a person wants to do what is pleasing to God, physical needs must be dealt with. And physical things become spiritual when they are shared. Take a piece of bread and eat it: that's a very physical act. Break it in half, eat half of it, and give half of it away, and the act becomes a very spiritual event. You've got your own house—you live in it, fix it up, jazz it up, put plush carpet in, hang some fancy drapes. Those are physical things which give you pleasure, enjoyment, and satisfaction. Open up the doors and invite in the world, a crowd of scraggly strangers from all over to walk on that carpet and see those new drapes—and that is a spiritual thing.

But because one cannot literally take in all the needy people of the world, there's another way to invite the stranger in. And that is to help build that stranger a simple, decent house in which to live. (See Isaiah 58:6–7.) We always say in Habitat for Humanity that we are doing a lot more than just building houses. We are building and seeking to be a part of building God's kingdom on earth. We are seeking to build relationships and challenging people to reach out and help others to share the love of Christ in very tangible ways as houses and community are built.

David Rowe describes this concept:

"We are God's people trying to do God's work as best we can. We treasure our participation in the kingdom of God as surely as Jesus knew we would treasure a pearl of great price. So we build, and we build, and we build. We build houses, we build communities, we build friendships, we build mailing lists, we build compassion. . . . We build amidst mountains of red tape, and frustration, and culture shock, and language difficulty, and personality conflicts, and financial crises, and homesickness, and jealousy. But still somehow we squeeze the love of Jesus into every joint."

Compartmentalized Church

Clyde Tilley, a member of our International Board of Directors and a Bible scholar, explains why the church and Habitat for Humanity are such good partners and why churches are seeing Habitat as a way to round out their own ministries:

> Christianity has suffered the violence of compartmentalization. We have separated the sacred from the secular. The church has become separated from the marketplace; the Sabbath, which belongs to God, from the work week which belongs to us; the tithe, which is God's, from the paycheck which is ours. . . .
>
> The gospel has been neatly divided into the personal gospel and the social gospel. The personal gospel is the Good News to the individual about salvation from sin. The social gospel is our Christian ministry to the structures of society . . . to make society more just and humane through the healing and minimization of human hurt. Too many conservatives or evangelicals have opted for the proclamation of the personal gospel. Too many liberals or mainliners have emphasized primarily the application of the social gospel. . . .
>
> [Yet] there is no social gospel and no personal gospel. There is only the Good News of and about Jesus Christ. It is the Good News of deliverance to the total person—physical, economic, social, spiritual. . . .
>
> It is unthinkable that Jesus would have sought to deliver people's "souls from sin" without at the same

time wishing to deliver them from physical disease, hunger, and ignorance. Likewise, it is unthinkable that Jesus would ever have ministered to people's physical needs merely to cultivate prospects for His "spiritual" ministry.

Habitat has captured the imagination and participation of a growing number and diversity of Christians. This is true, at least in part, because many have sensed in this ministry something strikingly Biblical and unmistakably holistic. . . . We are "a ministry performed by the total church through the proclamation of the total gospel for the benefit of total persons throughout the total world."

Clyde calls it "ministering with our hands for building, our mouths for speaking, our feet for going, as well as our minds for thinking, our money for erecting houses, as well as our pens for writing books. . . . We have a ministry to pocketbooks, both to those who have too little and to those who have too much. And whether one is poor or affluent, he or she has a ministry with total persons. Habitat never builds houses *for* the poor, rather *with* the poor. . . . Convinced that the poor need [more] co-workers [than] caseworkers, we work alongside them. In doing so the poor minister to us even as we minister to them."

Such true words. And that truth is at the heart of the successful partnership of Habitat and the church. A way is offered to reach out to people near and far with not just the words of Jesus, but His actions, too. Churches are the backbone of most Habitat projects, and the Covenant Church program is adding strength to the partnership, now and for the future.

11

Global Village

As a measuring stick for tough decisions, we use this philosophy: "A deal is a good deal only if it's a good deal for both sides."

Global Village certainly fits this criterion. It's a good deal for everyone, Global Village participants as well as Habitat for Humanity. It's a win-win type of a deal.

Global Village is the name of a new Habitat program that enables people to visit foreign lands for two to three weeks at minimal expense, experience different cultures first hand, and do something worthwhile. Many find it a way to combine true servanthood with travel and adventure.

The program works this way: Habitat affiliates, churches, campus chapters, and individuals from Europe, Australia, Japan, Canada, the United States, and other countries organize Global Village work camps to Habitat-sponsored projects in developing nations. The participants win because they gain extraordinary experiences not possible through regular tourist activities, and Habitat for Humanity wins because it gains short-term international partners to build houses and be effective spokespersons for the overseas projects when they return home.

For a number of years, work camps have been coming to Americus to help construct and renovate houses or assist with other tasks at Habitat headquarters. These groups have so much fun working and living together in Christian community, they hate to leave. What they find so meaningful is the close fellowship shared with each other, the nearby Habitat homeowners and Habitat community, and the unforgettable and oftentimes "eye-opening" experiences such excursions bring.

Having had their consciences raised by seeing poverty housing in Americus, work camp participants would often start Habitat affiliates back home. And it's also not uncommon for them to want to be involved in and supportive of our work around the globe.

So the same kind of work camps we've had in Americus began going to Habitat projects overseas. In the beginning, work camps were initiated by individuals and churches and received only limited support from Habitat headquarters. Invariably, the work camp folks returned filled with enthusiasm. And leaders of the projects where they had worked were equally pleased with the results.

Global Village

When we saw that these groups were doing so much good and gaining so much from it, we realized the great potential work camps had. That's how the idea for Global Village originated.[1] In 1988, the Global Village work camp program acquired its own full-time volunteer director in Americus and the ball was rolling.[2]

Global Village is about building partnerships and understanding around the world. Work camp groups consisting of ten to forty people work with Habitat for Humanity projects in remote jungle villages, inner city slums, and poor, dusty country communities. Participants pay their travel expenses as well as raise money for building materials prior to departure. Some of this money is raised through local churches or other organizations. Two weeks is the average length of stay for a Global Village work camp, with a slightly longer period for more distant destinations.

Participants work alongside local people to build houses with—and for—needy families. Each work camp has a well-chosen leader who is responsible for preparing the work campers through a multi-session orientation which teaches the vision of Habitat for Humanity and the purposes of the Global Village program. He or she also shares basic information about the country they will be visiting and working in.

Partnerships between Other Countries

One of the great benefits of the Global Village program is that it fosters cross-cultural understanding between North Americans and people of developing nations; it also is a means to create exciting international partnerships between other nations.

In mid-1989, Ploughshares, an organization of returned Peace Corps volunteers, teamed up with The Soviet Peace Fund and organized a unique group consisting of ten American and ten Soviet citizens. Calling themselves "U.S./Soviet Partners," they worked six weeks in earthquake-stricken Armenia followed by six weeks building Habitat houses in the Yakima Valley of Washington State. We, along with our daughter Georgia, joined the Partners for a week of work in Yakima.

At the same time these U.S./Soviet Partners were working together, a group from Tokyo Baptist Church in Japan was working with beneficiaries to build homes in Dumaguete City, Philippines. Another group from the "Drive for Youth" program in Great Britain committed to build homes in Kasulu, Tanzania. Other groups from the United States and Canada were organized for Peru, Costa Rica, the Dominican Republic, Guatemala, Uganda, South Africa, and India. Early in 1990, twenty-two volunteers from Australia joined seventeen others from North America to help build twenty houses in the Kusip region of Papua New Guinea.

First Global Village

Fourteen of these globe-trotting work camps were sent out from April 1989 to mid-January of the next year. All were such tremendous successes that we scheduled over forty more for 1990. And stories from participants tell us that Global Village is working.

One such story is from the first Global Village work camp held in the seaside village of Vila-Vila, Peru. Habitat staffer Tom Hall gave this moving account of his experiences:

> The warmth of the strong sun mixed with a cool Pacific sea breeze to form the perfect environment for a day's work not yet begun.

"Crew number four!" someone called out. My attention snapped, and . . . my eyes fell upon a Peruvian woman named Olivia whose Spanish flowed more with the turn of her hand than with her voice. She asked us to follow her. For crew number four, the Global Village work camp had begun.

First impressions are often for sharing, though what Olivia thought of me or I of her could not be shared—we simply did not have language enough to do so. With hand motions and eye contact, she taught me to mix mortar, to lay it in a neat and uniform thickness where a block would go, to dampen the blocks and hand them to her for correct placement on what soon became a straight and plumb wall . . . . I thought she was the homeowner of this house, and it felt good to be working alongside her, block by block, learning from her.

[Then] break time brought not only a cool drink but insight. One of our work campers whose Spanish allowed her the luxury of easy communication came over to see how we were doing. Through her, I learned that Olivia was not the new homeowner, but instead a Habitat homeowner from Arequipa, Peru, who had traveled 300 miles to be here.

Thankfully, God sends Olivias into our world to teach us, and I learned many things. For one, people with impressive job titles don't necessarily build good houses—it takes a good mason for that. Also, all of us have something to give. As little of this world's goods as Olivia had, she gave more to the building of that house than I did.

The next group, led by Habitat International Board member Mel West of Columbia, Missouri, went to Esparza, Costa Rica. Mel shares his experiences:

Tuesday, June 20 [1989], when we arrived at Esparza, we went down a steep hill to see a project where some of us would work. There, we met a woman named Lidia and her family, all of whom were living in a dirt-floored hovel. When it rained, water from the steep hillside ran through the house. The roof leaked badly. The walls were scraps of wood and tin. No real doors or windows existed, and the floor sloped with the hillside.

Lidia met us at the house and we fumbled to establish a relationship. She was almost in a state of shock as fourteen "gringos" descended upon her home, intent upon tearing it down. We did not know yet quite how to greet her. We were also in a state of shock over the magnitude of the task of leveling that hillside with pick and shovel for the purpose of building a decent house there.

But the work began. The local project director entered into a long discussion with International Partner Kay Spofford and the homeowner about the location of the building. Some of our group devised a plan for diverting the hillside water around the house. Materials were delivered, and volunteers dug ton upon ton of dirt away and moved it in wheelbarrows and buckets. Volunteers also mixed concrete by hand, poured footings, and laid block. Only simple tools were available.

The heat and humidity made for hard work, but somehow we all managed to "lift a house into the air" on that site. Relationships began to develop. Timid handshakes turned into smiles and hugs. Communication took place despite language barriers, and skills were shared.

Thursday night, nine days after our arrival, the local group held a celebration for us. Lidia and her family were there, as well as others who had been involved in the work. All barriers of language, education, income, religion, race, and culture disappeared as we ate, drank, danced, and celebrated together. We were all indeed brothers and sisters in Christ. A group of gringos, many of whom knew very little about Habitat, went to Costa Rica for two weeks and came back with a first-hand understanding of how Christian self-development mission works. We had grabbed shovels, picks, hammers, and wheelbarrows, and had worked in partnership with people of another country. . . .

Costa Ricans received strangers into their community and into their houses, and learned that Habitat is not just money from the USA, but that it is persons willing to get hot and dirty and tired with them.

On June 20 we stood with Lidia beside a shack, not sure how to build relationships or how to build her house. On June 29, with her house rising into the air, we danced together in celebration, not just for the house built but especially for the community built. That is Habitat for Humanity! It works!

Global Village in India

On the first Global Village work camp to India, headed by David Rowe, was Rick Hathaway, Habitat's new affiliate director. Rick shared portions of his Global Village trip in the October 1989 issue of *Habitat World:*

Thirty-three work campers representing 11 states from Vermont to California took love to their sisters and brothers in India. . . . Ranging from 14 to 65 years old, group members gathered at Boston's Logan Airport. . . . A two-day journey brought us to the city of Bombay on the shore of the Arabian Sea. This city of nearly 8 million attracts people from villages all over the country, each in search of hope and prosperity. Still, over 50 percent live in destitution in dwellings of 100 to 200 square feet constructed of scrap metal, plastic, paper, and other materials that Westerners might consider garbage. The courage of these people is astounding. Amid open sewer trenches, residents go about their daily tasks with hope and joy.

When we arrived, Bombay Habitat for Humanity was still weeks away from beginning construction, so the work camp visited the project area, meeting with partner families. We sang with the children, shared in prayer, and had our spirits lifted. . . .

Our work camp divided into two groups, one traveling to Hubli where that project's first six houses were in progress, the other to Khammam, where over 250 homes have been built to date.

At Hubli, work campers and community members led by Chris Fabian, a New Hampshire high school student and veteran of Habitat House-Raising Walk '88, dug foundations with picks and shovels. Chris and his brother Mark were accompanied by their parents, Rick and Georgene Fabian, former Peace Corps volunteers who had served in south India some years before.

V.G. Raj, an older boy in the community, helped work camper Mike Conner shop through a chaotic Hubli bazaar. Emily Diamond, another work camper, was invited to speak to a group of teachers at a local school. And the one-mile walk to the work site each day was a great opportunity to talk with curious school children, watch women weaving mats, and to feel the love and concern which is ever-present among the people of Hubli.

Lepers Housed

We learned that one of the workers, Doris Poole, a veteran of two India work camps, had first journeyed to Khammam with a Habitat work group in 1987. During that trip, she had visited a village of twenty-two families, all of whom were afflicted with Hansen's Disease (leprosy). When she returned two years later, she was very excited to find each of these families living in decent shelter.

Doris remembers the first time she went with David Rowe to visit the colony. When the tour was over, the head man of the village grabbed David with his stumps and said something to him in the Telegu language. The interpreter, momentarily distracted, did not translate what he said. So, still clinging to David's hands, he repeated the statement. This time the interpreter turned to David, "What he said is, 'We can work. We can work.'" And now they all have houses.

On this second visit, David was also moved by what had happened in the leper colony: "Certainly one of the high points of this work camp was to take our people back to the village and be shown the homes that those people with stumps for hands and feet, those people with the world's greatest stigma attached to them, the outcast of thousands and thousands of years, had helped to build themselves. These men and women and children with Hansen's Disease had a mind to work."

Ministry to Our Young People

David also shared something else very significant about the India work camp: "We took ten teenagers between the ages of 13 and 19 (one college kid, three high school seniors, and a bunch of 13-year-olds). Taking these ten kids out of suburban America over to India for three weeks and experiencing life in India [was] seeing those kids just come alive. I don't think there was anybody in our group who did better, who had better health, who worked harder, who was better at simply relating and loving people in India than those young people. I think what Habitat is providing as an opportunity for ministry to young people across America is one of the greatest gifts, but we don't talk about it much. We talk about our ministry to the affluent. We talk about a ministry with the poor, but we are doing some things very significant in the lives of young people as well."

David likens every Global Village work camp to a Sunday school class. He feels strongly that his group's experience in India was three and a half weeks of worship, three and a half weeks of prayer, three and a half weeks of taking humble and unprofessional hands and lifting them up to the Lord. "And lo and behold," he points out, "once we lifted up our hands, we found that there are some Indian people with far greater skills than we had who were willing to hold our hands and lead us to make something significant of our time there in India."

An Emotional Farewell

Ted Swisher, director of Habitat for Humanity of Australia and a member of the first Global Village work camp to Papua New Guinea, wrote about the dramatic conclusion of the experience: "After six hard days of work the twenty houses were completed and the traditional Habitat house dedication ceremony was held. The dedication consisted of two segments: 1) presentation of a Bible to each homeowner family by the work campers; and 2) presentation of a *belum* (the Papua New Guinea woven carrying bag) filled with tropical fruit to each work camper by the homeowners.

"In these exchanges, the emotions of the week were vented in hugs and tears, as everyone rejoiced in the oneness that was experienced but mourned the parting that was to come. After an especially tearful exchange between work campers and homeowners, a local teacher who was officiating also broke down but managed amidst the weeping to say that this was the first time [he'd ever witnessed] that white people had allowed themselves to cry in front of black people.

"After the dedication ceremony, the Americans and Australians were honored by a 'sing-sing.' This unique celebration lasted all night and concluded with the villagers and work campers walking up the mountain to the road for a final farewell."

A Concept That Works

Global Village participants have made the decision that they need to be about the Lord's business with their hands. They've decided that they're going to lift up their hands or reach out their hands or dig the earth with their hands as a part of their worship and prayer life.

Helping each other—learning from each other. Global

Village is peace-making in action. And as we watch work camp after work camp go overseas and as we listen to their stories and marvel at how their trips produce such life-changing results for them and for the people they work with, we know that Global Village is a concept that works, a concept that helps us all.

The invisible homeless in
Nicaragua . . .

Pakistan.

Zaire . . .

Storage shed was former
residence of Habitat partner
family in Cartersville,
Georgia . . .

Rosie Brown's old house —
Coahoma, Mississippi.

Rosie helps nail trusses
together as part of her sweat
equity.

Inside her cold shack, Rosie
dreams about the kitchen
cabinets and indoor plumbing
she will have in her well-
insulated Habitat home.

Campus Chapters members
working in the Coahoma
Collegiate Challenge in
Coahoma, Mississippi, 1990

Campus Chapters students
raise walls on Rosie's new
house (Campus Chapters
Director David McDaniels [left]
coordinated twenty-six chapters
that built six houses in six weeks.)

(Ray Scioscia photos).

Second annual "University of Richmond Century Bike Race" — Tony Green, child of Habitat home owner, with his sister, cutting ribbon at beginning of women's race. This Campus Chapter event raised $22,000 (David Eastis photo).

Debby Marx, her husband, Terry, and their three children moved into their new Habitat home Thanksgiving 1989. Debby is painting walls of McGill's Habitat home under construction at the same time as hers.

Dumaguete City, Philippines, awaits arrival of first Global Village Work Camp in 1989. New Habitat homes shown at left (Kevin Duffus photo).

Global Village Work Camp in Esparza, Costa Rica.

III

---

*Building Excitement
for the Future*

12

Habitat on the Move

As we began the 1990s, Habitat for Humanity had projects in nearly 500 American cities and towns and in more than eighty locations in twenty-nine other countries.

Those figures will sound more amazing when you know that we began the 1980s with only eleven projects in the United States and five in three other nations.

In 1980, Habitat projects built 120 houses. In 1990 we expect to build that many *every ten days*. That's more than 4,000 annually. By 1994, we expect to be building not 4,000 but 10,000 houses a year!

And what about by the end of the century? By the year 2000, the twenty-fourth anniversary of this movement, we expect to have projects in 2,000 cities and in sixty countries—and we expect to be building at least 20,000 houses a year. *Twenty thousand!*

What is it about this little idea which originated in rural Georgia that has made it explode on the world scene? What has caused a program that took three months to build its first house to grow to a point where it is building one house every daylight hour of every day?

Those houses don't build themselves. So we really should be asking: What has attracted tens of thousands of people to the work, inspiring them to labor for low pay or no pay to build houses for poor people they didn't even know?

Common Thread

Different people will give different answers to these questions, but there are two common threads running through them all. They are the threads of vision and common sense.

From the beginning, we have had a vision which, we believe, is from heaven. It is expressed clearly in the Bible, in Deuteronomy 15:4: "There shall be no poor among you, since the Lord will surely bless you in the land which the Lord your God is giving you as an inheritance to possess" (NASB).

This scripture states the ideal. God desires the needs of all His people to be met. No one should be poor in God's order of things.

But we all know there were poor people in the days of the Bible and we still have poor today. Well, God tells us what to do: "If there is a poor man among your brothers in any of the towns of the land that the Lord your God is giving you, do not be hardhearted or tightfisted toward your poor brother. Rather be openhanded and freely lend him whatever he needs" (Deuteronomy 15:7–8, NIV).

And that is what Habitat does.

One of the most visible signs of poverty is poor housing or no housing. And it tears at the hearts of caring people to see fellow human beings living like animals. They want to do something because we are all made in the image of God, and it is God's basic nature to give. So, when people see fellow humans suffering they want to respond and they want to do it in a way that really makes a difference.

What Habitat Offers Makes Sense

Habitat for Humanity offers a way to get involved that makes sense, a way which allows people to give as an expression of their faith. Building a house for a needy family, working with them, and then having the family move in and pay the money back on terms they can afford—no profit, no interest—the Bible finance plan seems so right, both from a common-sense standpoint and from scripture. It enables all kinds of folks to work together and feel good about it. Faith is being put into practice and something practical and tangible is coming out of it.

A Bold Vision

When we first started talking about this idea—to eliminate poverty housing and homelessness in the world—people laughed at us, but we did get their attention. A vision, boldly stated, cannot be ignored.

The Bible tells us that without a vision the people perish. In the absence of a dream, an idea dies. So this is what we do. Habitat partners nurture that vision in projects all over the country and around the world, teaching people that the goal can be for their town, their city. The goal is to eliminate poverty housing and homelessness in their area. Another goal is also nurtured— that each project will not only build as many houses as possible, but will also be a conscience to the local community, saying over and over and over—poverty housing and homelessness are unacceptable.

Radical Common Sense

Such thinking may seem radical, but it is also eminent common sense. Millard was once introduced to speak by a college student who said, "I'd like to introduce you to a man who deals in radical common sense. Someone who presents an idea that works. An idea that shows that by sharing the time on our hands, the love in our hearts, and the belief in our souls, we can heal the housing problems of the world."

This young man put his finger on many of the fundamental reasons why people are attracted to Habitat for Humanity. First, the vision of Habitat is radical. Eliminate poverty housing and homelessness everywhere? You've got to be kidding! Haven't you read the statistics? And yet, it is common sense to propose that everyone who gets sleepy at night should have a good and decent place to sleep.

Even Habitat's "finance plan" devised to be affordable to those with low incomes is common sense. No profit and no interest, coupled with sweat equity, make it possible for poor people to afford monthly house payments.

Simple Idea

Somebody once said that Americans will support anything they can take a picture of. We have certainly found that to be true in Habitat for Humanity. We're sure Habitat houses are the most photographed houses in the world. People take pictures of them and generously support the work. Habitat is a practical, tangible venture that people can see and comprehend.

The idea is so simple. Just find people who are too poor to go to the bank. They live in deplorable, substandard housing and need a decent place to live. Habitat says yes to these people when no one else will. "Yes, we'll build a simple house with you and then you can pay the money back at no profit and no interest. Yes, we'll recycle your house payments to build more houses. Then you, the homeowners, will become full partners with other Habitat folks and the work will keep expanding." And it is music to their ears.

Government Alone Cannot Fix It

Another reason Habitat for Humanity is on the move is that more and more of us realize that government alone cannot fix the problem of the poor. Only a massive effort from everyone—government and the private sector—can succeed in doing what God has commanded: Get rid of poverty. "There shall be no poor among you!" No shacks. No poverty housing of any kind. No homelessness.

Demilitarized Building Zone

And what's even more exciting is how different people are melding into one furious building "unit," working together. Habitat for Humanity is increasingly proving to be a neutral, "demilitarized" zone where Baptists, United Methodists, Pentecostals, Catholics, liberals, conservatives, and others can meet and work together, hammering out faith and praises to God as more and more houses go up. The "theology of the hammer" is an idea whose time has come.

Spreading around the Globe

And the work is spreading to more and more places all the time. We, along with International Board Member LeRoy Troyer, visited Soviet Armenia in July 1989 and found a tremendous interest there in forming a Habitat for Humanity project. Habitat hopes to launch work in that Soviet Republic.

A group is currently forming a Habitat for Humanity project in England. Another one is forming in New Zealand.

Proposals are being drawn up to launch projects in Swaziland, Zimbabwe, and Namibia. There is strong interest in several South American countries where we are not yet building. And there is also interest in Israel, Poland, China, and Japan.

And in countries where there are already projects, the work is expanding rapidly. In Australia, where the seed for Habitat for Humanity was first planted in late 1987 when Millard was asked to visit there, the idea is taking firm root. Official Habitat projects have been approved in Adelaide, Melbourne, Sydney, and Wollongong.

Jimmy Carter will lead over a thousand volunteers to put up a hundred houses in a week of intense building in Tijuana, Mexico in June 1990. In late October 1989 he spoke at a fundraising dinner in San Diego which raised more than half a million dollars for that project, and for the work in San Diego (where seven houses will be built during the same week).

In the Mezquital Valley, ninety miles northeast of Mexico City, a thousand houses are being built in fifty villages in 1990 alone! This is the largest single project ever attempted by Habitat for Humanity in one year. The houses cost from $854 to $1,700 each.

In the beleaguered nation of Nicaragua, Habitat has been building houses since 1984. The work is expanding in the western, central, and northern parts of the country. And now the building of 500 houses in the Bluefields area of eastern Nicaragua has been approved to help the people respond to a recent devastating hurricane. All of us in Habitat remain dedicated to our work in this needy land and expect it to continue growing in the years ahead.

In Peru, under the committed leadership of Zenon Colque Rojas, a total of forty houses a month were being built by early 1990 in five locations, and soon construction will start in seven more cities. By 1992, we expect to be putting up eight houses a day—a house an hour during the work day—or a total of nearly 3,000 houses a year in that one country.

The excitement about Habitat for Humanity in Peru is

fantastic. In April 1989 Millard and the Board of Directors of Habitat for Humanity International met in Arequipa, Peru, followed by a tour of Habitat projects in Arequipa, Juliaca, Puno, and Vila-Vila. Everywhere the delegation went they were met by hundreds of Habitat homeowners, prospective homeowners, and friends, throwing confetti and flowers, yelling and waving, so full of enthusiasm they could hardly contain themselves.

In India, Habitat projects are building ten houses a month in the state of Andra Pradesh and new projects are getting under way in three other parts of the country, including Bombay, surely one of the neediest cities on earth.

In Zaire, where our family lived and worked from 1973 until mid-1976, the work continues to expand. Over a thousand houses have been built in thirty locations. In the coming decade, the number of locations will at least double and the number of houses will quadruple.

The story is the same in country after country where Habitat is working. The idea has taken hold in the hearts and minds of people and they are responding.

Growing at Home

And of course, here at home and in Canada, Habitat is on the move as never before. New projects are starting at the rate of a new city every two to three days! The interest and excitement are truly awesome. And, as with the overseas work, the existing projects are gaining strength.

Habitat folks in Charlotte, North Carolina, will complete their one hundredth house in 1990. They've gotten the whole city fired up about the work and committed to eliminating poverty housing there as soon as possible. On October 14, 1989, more than 700 people came out to put up five houses in a day.

Atlanta Habitat is also close to finishing a hundred houses and there is a little friendly competition between the Charlotte and Atlanta projects. On the same Saturday that Charlotte Habitat put up five houses, Atlanta Habitat started nine houses, which were completely finished in six successive Saturdays. Jacksonville, Florida, only affiliated since 1988, expects to build ten houses in 1990 and twice that many in 1991.

Following the natural disasters of Hurricane Hugo and the California earthquake in late 1989, Habitat projects in South Carolina and Santa Cruz County, California have geared up to build more houses than ever before.

The small town of Winkler in southern Manitoba formed the first Habitat project in Canada in 1986. The group's first house was completed and dedicated early the next year. Since then, building has continued at a regular pace, and five more projects have been started in Manitoba and Ontario. Several other cities, including some in the western and maritime provinces, are in the process of launching new affiliates as this book goes to press.

Do Older Projects Lose Steam?

One of the most thrilling things about Habitat is that the older projects are doing so well. People are not running out of steam. They're just as excited ten or eleven years later as they were at the start, and that seems impossible when you think about the normally high drop-out rate of volunteers.

But it's true. San Antonio, Texas, was the first project started in the United States outside of Georgia. By mid-1990 that affiliate had twenty-four houses completed and occupied and their tempo of building was steadily increasing.

Immokalee, Florida, Habitat was begun soon after San Antonio's project. In January 1989, we helped this Florida group dedicate house number fifty and roof number fifty-one. By mid-1990, the number of completed houses was sixty-four, and another half dozen were under construction.

Kansas City, Missouri, Habitat, begun in October 1979, set a goal to build fifty houses by 1989. On November 12 of that year, they had a big celebration. House number fifty was under construction. Early in the new year it was complete and occupied and several more houses were underway. This on-the-move project plans to build at least a hundred more houses over the coming decade.

The story is the same all across the land. Some projects build faster than others. Some prefer blitz campaigns. Others just plod along week after week. Of course, there are discouragements, setbacks, and very real disappointments. Sometimes there's not enough money. Sometimes, leadership problems. But, we all keep going, in the firm conviction that God has called us to this noble task.

Groups Moving Us On

A major reason Habitat for Humanity is growing so quickly and constantly is that more and more churches, companies, other organizations, and individuals are getting involved.

The covenant church program continues to expand in amazing ways. And churches are reporting wonderful things that happen as a result of building Habitat houses, as described in Chapter 10. Jo Morrison, a Habitat leader in eastern Tennessee and a member of a covenant church, says, "The churches are feeling a sense of revival and accomplishment."

Corporate Sponsorship Program

One of our most exciting new developments is something the Southern Bell Company, headquartered in Atlanta, is pioneering—a *Corporate Sponsorship Program*. In an agreement signed with Habitat, the company established a cooperative relationship with the objective of providing affordable housing for low-income families and making decent shelter a matter of conscience.

The specific aims of corporate participation are to:

• Provide resources of industry to a well-established nonprofit endeavor.

• Encourage employee volunteer activities with Habitat for Humanity.

• Provide financial support for local Habitat for Humanity affiliates.

• Raise the level of awareness about the work of Habitat for Humanity.

• Underscore company commitment to communities they serve.

Under terms of the agreement with Southern Bell, the company provides partial funding for "Southern Bell Teams" that build houses with local affiliates. The teams, made up of

Southern Bell employees, do fund-raising on their own to add to the money given by the company. (The company portion is usually 25 percent of the cost of a house.) On their own time, these company people work with local affiliates to build houses for low-income families.[1]

In late 1989 the Fieldstone Company in Orange County, California, entered into an agreement with the local Habitat affiliate to help build forty-eight houses in 1990. The company is donating the forty-eight lots, putting up a $2 million no-interest loan and providing the necessary building experts to direct the actual construction of the houses.

Fieldstone was inspired to undertake this ambitious project after a couple of its executives saw the video, "The Excitement is Building," which shows the construction of the twenty houses in a week in Atlanta by the Jimmy Carter Work Project. What especially inspired them was the commitment of the John Wieland Company to build six of those twenty houses that week in Atlanta as its contribution to the effort. The Wieland Company continued its commitment to Atlanta Habitat by building three more houses in 1989.

The Ben Franklin Savings and Loan Association of Portland, Oregon, has donated nine houses to Portland Habitat for Humanity. That local affiliate is renovating those houses for resale to low-income families.

John Bontreger, president and founder of Signature Inns, headquartered in Indianapolis, Indiana, got turned on to Habitat for Humanity at the Carter Work Project in Charlotte in 1987. Since then, he has joined the Board of Directors of Indianapolis Habitat for Humanity and has raised enough money for two houses in that city with a company golf tournament.

The Jaycees in Greensboro, North Carolina, also had a golf tournament that raised $50,000 for that local affiliate. Millard was there when they broke ground in October 1989 for a six-house project which has been dubbed "Jaycees Habitat for Humanity"!

As this book goes to press in May 1990, three other organizations are becoming significantly involved in helping Habitat for Humanity: Insteel Construction Systems of Brunswick, Georgia,

The Muzquiz Group of Tijuana, Mexico and *Builder Magazine,* the official publication of the National Association of Home Builders. Insteel contributed their innovative 3–D wall panels for ten houses in Tijuana for the Carter Work Project in June 1990 and for one Habitat house in Brunswick. The Muzquiz Group contributed generously to the Habitat project in Tijuana by providing site preparation, engineering, and building materials. *Builder Magazine* officials presented a $5000 check to President Carter, Bob Wilson, coordinator of the Carter Work Projects, and the two of us at the Carter Center in Atlanta on April 26, 1990, and announced their goal to raise $100,000 for Habitat through a newly created "Builder Fund Helping Habitat for Humanity."

And the list goes on and on. . . .[2]

International Headquarters

In the international headquarters in Americus, plans are being made to deal with the growth which lies ahead. The main office complex covers a city block, built almost entirely by volunteers. In nearby neighborhoods, there are twenty-five houses to accommodate over 170 volunteers who do most of the work at the headquarters. And more than 120 people are employed, including personnel in Americus and the regional offices.

Both the number of volunteers and paid personnel will have to be increased in the months ahead. This will mean a need for more office space, but additional offices are already scheduled to be built. It's a great problem to have.

Habitat has twelve regional centers in the United States, a national center with three regional offices in Canada, a national center in Australia, and several in developing nations. (See Appendix B for a full listing of all these offices.) God has blessed this ministry tremendously with dynamic leaders in each of these locations.

In 1989, LeRoy Troyer chaired a long-range planning committee of the Board of Directors which mapped out a reorganization of our staff in Americus and set in motion a five-year plan which will be updated every year—because Habitat is expanding that quickly.

Faith, Hope, Love, Dreams, Miracles

So Habitat for Humanity is on the move. Building thousands of houses. Involving thousands upon thousands of people. But a few simple words capture the essence of what it's all about:

Faith. Hope. Love. Dreams. Miracles.

Faith is not really faith until it's acted upon. Then it comes alive. It means something. Habitat is enabling people to take concrete steps of faith. And it's blessing people, giver and receiver alike.

Hope is intangible, but it is real. If it is present in a life, there is joy and peace. Where there is no hope, there is no joy, no laughter, no future. Habitat brings hope and with it, great joy.

Love makes anything grow. It surely makes those involved in Habitat for Humanity blossom and expand their horizons in so many ways.

And then dreams and miracles. We have had the joyous experience of participating in literally hundreds of dedication services for Habitat houses all around the world. Tears flow freely everywhere. Laughter abounds. Faith, hope, and love are talked about with deep emotion. But what get mentioned most of all are dreams and miracles. A simple house is a dream come true for so many, an impossible dream most of us take for granted. "My own house? We are going to have our own house? It has to be a miracle." That is what we hear time and time again.

We'll never forget Evelyn Jackson in Atlanta talking about dreams coming true. It was Friday afternoon on the last day of the Carter project. The houses were finished and we were all gathered on some vacant lots across the street to give the keys to the new homeowners. Evelyn was one of the homeowners chosen to speak for the families. She started by thanking all the volunteers and expressing in a rush of words that the houses were like a miracle, getting built so fast by the dedicated volunteers. But when she said, "These houses are all of our dreams, . . . ," she choked up. Her eyes filled with tears. Evelyn struggled to compose herself. She had something important to say and she wanted to get it out. Finally, she started over and with a big, big, smile, she finished the message she so wanted to express. She exclaimed, with joy and love and hope in her words: "These houses are all of our dreams for tomorrow come true." Her talk was recorded and it became the emotional high point of the video, "The Excitement is Building." So her message of faith and love and dreams and miracles has blessed literally thousands of people all across the land.

"Dreams for tomorrow." We can't help but think again about ten-year-old Tomorrow Tucker who now lives in one of those simple, decent houses in Atlanta and who can now dream those dreams Evelyn so eloquently articulated.

Hope for tomorrow. Dreams coming true. A miracle of God's love.

A Drop in the Bucket

Some skeptics say that what is being done is but a speck on the horizon. We may talk about thousands of houses, but millions are needed. This work is but a "drop in the bucket" in the face of overwhelming poverty.

But if we had believed those who laughed at our idea years ago, think of all the people who would not have houses as you read this.

We can change things. *You* can change things. By God's power and love, all of us can make a difference. And Habitat for Humanity will increasingly change things for the better in the years to come as more and more people, churches, businesses, foundations, other groups, and governments are inspired to help the poor have adequate shelter; as Habitat stands firm by the principles and methods which have served so well for the first fourteen years; and as we all stay with our simple formula of no-profit, no-interest, faith-motivated, Christ-centered, building of simple, but solid and good houses for—and with—God's people in need.

"Dreams for tomorrow," Evelyn Jackson said.

So, today, right now, it is time to get our hammers, saws, trowels, levels, shovels, and wheelbarrows. We've got new houses to put up and others to renovate and repair.

The Excitement Is Building!

Habitat for Humanity is on a roll, literally, as five houses donated by the College of Wooster in Ohio, are moved to their new site to be renovated and sold to low-income families (Mike Shenk photo, courtesy *Daily Record*, Wooster, Ohio).

Before: After it was purchased from the city of Bridgeport, Connecticut, for $1, this house was transformed by the labor of hundreds of people.

After: Helen and Jose Montalvo, with their three sons, are the proud owners. All decorative woodwork was either refurbished or replaced.

Appropriate technology builds Habitat houses in Assinman, Ghana, W. Africa. Blocks are made using a "TEK" Block Press. This method of making blocks reduces the amount of cement and sand needed since the clay in the soil acts as a binder and filler.

Wood Miser sawmill in operation near Bluefields, Nicaragua.

1989 House-Raising Week in Winnipeg, Manitoba, Canada. Volunteers hammer together stud walls for two houses built for Lopez and Och families.

Millard Fuller bids farewell to children's choir who sang at house dedication for "wheelies" (disabled) in Port Moresby, Papua New Guinea.

Val Wagner, a blind man, plays accordion while Habitat homeowners in Winnipeg, Manitoba, Canada, sing during House-Raising Week 1989. Left to right: Val Wagner, Angela Och (homeowner of one of the houses being constructed), Mrs. Maria Lopez (another homeowner of the other house built during work week), and her daughters Sonia, Gloria and son, Wilson.

The joyous result of Habitat partnerships! Doris Cousins moves in on Valentine's Day 1990 to the third completed house by Richmond Metropolitan Habitat for Humanity (Mark Fagerburg photo).

Belo Horizonte, Brazil. Neat rows of Habitat houses with tile roofs.

Habitat is not only building houses but entire neighborhoods (Ray Scioscia photo).

Celebration/
Blitz–Building, 1991

On the weekend of September 26–28, 1991, there will be a huge gathering in Columbus, Ohio, to celebrate the first fifteen years of this movement. Thousands of people will come together from Habitat projects all over the world. The Fifteenth Anniversary Celebration is going to be incredible!

And an event leading up to the celebration will be equally incredible. Starting in June, fifteen weeks prior to the celebration, fifteen different work teams will start blitz-building at points on the perimeter of the United States. A couple of the teams will start outside the United States—one in Canada and one in Mexico. Other teams will start in places like Miami, Florida; Portland, Maine; San Diego, California; and Seattle, Washington. Each week these building teams will travel to another city or cities in the direction of Columbus, Ohio. They will stop at the city limits, join local builders there, parade to the construction site, and blitz-build houses for a week. And they'll do this for fifteen weeks.

All Fifty States

During that time, we expect to build in all fifty states as well as Mexico and Canada. (Simultaneously, other traveling blitz-building teams will be on the move, building along the way, in other countries where Habitat is working.)

In all, we will raise $15 million and blitz-build 1,500 houses, getting as many as possible completely finished and others far enough along so that local people can complete them soon thereafter.

On September 26, the builders will assemble at various points around Columbus and then march into the city for the beginning of the celebration, pushing wheelbarrows and carrying hammers, saws, and other building tools in a dramatic demonstration of what can be accomplished when God's people get organized and have a mind to work.

The traditional "Habitation," the highlight of the celebration, will be at St. John Arena of Ohio State University on Friday evening, September 27. All other celebration activities will be at the Ohio Expositions Center.

Want to Participate?

If you would like to participate in this exciting event, call or write the International Headquarters in Americus:

> Director
> Fifteenth Anniversary Blitz-Building Campaign
>   and Celebration
> Habitat for Humanity International, Inc.
> Habitat and Church Streets
> Americus, GA 31709–3498
> 912–924–6935
> Fax: 912–924–6541

Notes

Chapter 1

1. The full story is told in *The Cotton Patch Evidence* by Dallas Lee, published in 1971 by Harper & Row.

2. The three books already published are *Bokotola* (1977) and *Love in the Mortar Joints* (1980), both by New Century Publishers, and *No More Shacks!* (1986) by Word Books.

3. Clarence Jordan died suddenly on October 29, 1969, while the Johnson house was still under construction.

4. The director of the 1986 Walk was Judi Carpenter of Indianapolis. She was assisted by a dedicated team of twelve volunteers who did all the planning for the event. Our son Chris served on the Walk team, prior to launching his career as a campus minister.

5. This $35,000 gift was part of the Charlotte Habitat's tithe for the international work. All Habitat affiliates are expected to give at least 10 percent of their undesignated income to Habitat International headquarters for the work in developing countries. On the average, a house in a Third World country costs 10 percent of what a Habitat house costs in the United States and Canada.

6. This moving talk by Evelyn Jackson and the full story of both Jimmy Carter Work Projects in 1988—in Atlanta and Philadelphia—and the House-Raising Walk are on a video made by Habitat for Humanity entitled, "The Excitement is Building."

Chapter 2

1. "Theology of the hammer" is explained in detail in a chapter by that title in Millard's book, *No More Shacks!*

2. The policy of Habitat for Humanity is not to accept government funds (tax money) for the building or renovation of houses or for administrative expenses. Government grants, loans, or direct gifts of land, old houses to be remodeled, or the constructing of streets, sidewalks, utilities, etc.—setting the stage to build—we consider acceptable provided no strings are attached that violate Habitat principles.

Chapter 3

1. Both of these goals were to raise extra money, i.e., above the amount raised in previous years. In 1984, the total money raised for all of our work was $3.5 million. The goal was to increase this amount by $10 million over the next two years.

Chapter 4

1. A more complete account of what life was like for the Hyde family in their old house is found in *No More Shacks!,* pages 178 and 179.

Chapter 5

1. See Appendix B.

Chapter 6

1. When houses are blitz-built, the homeowner families put in their additional sweat equity hours on other houses built either before or after the blitz-built ones.

2. Habitat for Humanity International, Heifer Project International, and The American Bible Society.

Chapter 7

1. All International Partners who have served abroad with Habitat for Humanity are listed in Appendix F. As of mid-1990, there were more than 100 International Partners serving in overseas Habitat projects.

Chapter 8

1. The National Coalition for the Homeless estimates the number of homeless in the U.S. to be 3,000,000.

2. *USA Today* article, "Homeless: 14 million on 'edge,'" August 9, 1989.

3. The house was built by Spokane Habitat for Humanity and sold, at no profit and no interest, to another local nonprofit group, Spokane Neighborhood Centers, which is operating the facility. Millard was present and spoke when the transitional house was dedicated on April 23, 1990.

Chapter 9

1. See Appendix C.

Chapter 10

1. *Yearbook of American and Canadian Churches,* 1989 edition.
2. For further information, contact Vision Habitat at our Americus, Georgia, headquarters.
3. For the full story of Koinonia Partnership Housing and our three years in Zaire, Africa, read *Bokotola* and *Love in the Mortar Joints.*
4. Habitat International Board member Warren Sawyer of Swampscott, Massachusetts, proposed the Covenant Church program to the International Board of Directors in 1987.

Chapter 11

1. The Global Village concept was developed at a planning conference of the International department of Habitat, held in Oberlin, Ohio, in 1987. This conference was hosted by former Habitat International board member, Bill Clarke, of Canton, Ohio.
2. The first director of the Global Village program was Karen Foreman, who had served as an International Partner in Zaire.

Chapter 12

1. In April, 1990, an agreement was signed with the BMA Company of Greenville, South Carolina, for a second corporate sponsorship program. This fine company works with independent building supply dealers in more than 800 cities.
2. A brand new program, "Habitat for Humanity—Recreational Vehicles," is being coordinated by Jack and Lois Wolters. People with RV's, who want to work on Habitat projects, should write to Lois Wolters, Rt. 1, Box 442, Columbus, North Carolina, 28722. (An RV park is being built in Americus at the International Headquarters, as this book goes to press.)

Appendix A

The Mission, Purposes, Guidelines, and Goal of Habitat for Humanity International, Inc.

Mission:

Habitat for Humanity works in partnership with God and people everywhere, from all walks of life, to develop communities with God's people in need by building and renovating houses so that there are decent houses in decent communities in which people can live and grow into all that God intended.

Purposes:

The official purposes of Habitat for Humanity are to sponsor specific projects in Habitat development globally, by constructing modest but adequate housing, and to associate with other organizations functioning with purposes consistent with those of Habitat, as stated in the Articles of Incorporation, namely:

1. To witness to the Gospel of Jesus Christ throughout the world by working in cooperation with God's people in need to create a better habitat in which to live and work.
2. To work in cooperation with other agencies and groups which have a kindred purpose.
3. To witness to the Gospel of Jesus Christ through loving acts and the spoken and written word.
4. To enable an expanding number of persons from all walks of life to participate in this ministry.

Guidelines for implementing the above purposes are as follows:

1. Believing that the work of Habitat for Humanity is inspired by the Holy Spirit, we understand the purposes express the hope that others may be grasped and led in yet unforeseen ministries by the Holy Spirit.
2. "Adequate housing" as used in the purposes means

housing, and much more, and includes total environment, e.g., economic development, compassionate relationships, health, energy development, etc.

3. The term "in cooperation" used in Habitat's stated purposes should be defined in terms of partnership:

    a. Partnership implies the right of all parties to engage in vigorous negotiation and the development of mutually agreed-upon goals and procedures. The negotiation in partnership should occur with each project and will include such items as defining what adequate housing means in that particular project, who are God's needy, and what local entity will control the project.

    b. Partnership further implies that all project personnel—local people or International Partners—have a primary and equal relationship to the local Habitat committee in regard to all matters relating to that particular project.

4. Habitat's position is one of responding to expressed needs of a people in a given area who are seeking a relationship of partner with Habitat for Humanity. A primary concern in all matters is respect for persons, including their culture, visions, and dignity.

5. All Habitat projects must establish a Fund for Humanity, and financing of houses and other ventures must be on a no-profit, no-interest basis. Each Fund for Humanity will be funded through voluntary gifts (in cash and in kind), grants, and interest-free loans, all from individuals, churches, other groups, and foundations. All repayments from houses or other Habitat-financed ventures will also be returned to the local Fund for Humanity. Finally, Habitat projects may operate enterprises which will generate funds for the local Fund for Humanity.

Goal:

The ultimate goal of Habitat for Humanity is to eliminate poverty housing and homelessness from the face of the earth by building basic but adequate housing. Furthermore, all our words and actions are for the purpose of putting shelter on the hearts and minds of people in such a way that poverty housing and homelessness become socially, politically, and religiously unacceptable in our nation and world.

Appendix B

Project Locations, Regional and National Centers
(as of April 1, 1990)

INTRODUCTION

Habitat for Humanity projects are either sponsored or affiliated. *Sponsored projects* receive both funds and personnel from Habitat International. *Affiliated projects* (located in U.S., Canada, Australia, and South Africa) follow Habitat for Humanity guidelines, but the responsibility for generating funds and recruiting personnel rests with a local committee. *Regional* and *national centers* assist the affiliated projects within their geographical region and help promote the worldwide work of Habitat.

HABITAT FOR HUMANITY WORLDWIDE

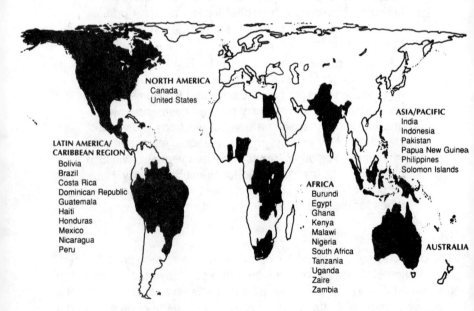

NORTH AMERICA
Canada
United States

LATIN AMERICA/ CARIBBEAN REGION
Bolivia
Brazil
Costa Rica
Dominican Republic
Guatemala
Haiti
Honduras
Mexico
Nicaragua
Peru

AFRICA
Burundi
Egypt
Ghana
Kenya
Malawi
Nigeria
South Africa
Tanzania
Uganda
Zaire
Zambia

ASIA/PACIFIC
India
Indonesia
Pakistan
Papua New Guinea
Philippines
Solomon Islands

AUSTRALIA

SPONSORED PROJECTS
LATIN AMERICA/CARIBBEAN REGION

LATIN AMERICA/CARIBBEAN
REGION (continued)

MEXICO

Tijuana

Anahuac

Huasteca

San Pedro Capula — Mezquital Valley
Dexthi Alberto

NICARAGUA

Jinotega Expansion

Mulukuku

Matagalpa
Tonola — Esquipulas
Nicaragua Expansion
German Pomares

Juigalpa

East Coast/
Bluefields

Ticuantepe

PERU

Juliaca
Mañazo — Puno
Arequipa
Vila-Vila — Tacna

AFRICA REGION

BURUNDI

Gitega

EGYPT

Cairo

GHANA

Asadame

Assinman — Breman Asikuma

AFRICA REGION (continued)

KENYA

Lubokha □ Ndabarnach
□ □ Nzoia Community

MALAWI

Lilongwe □

□ Zomba

NIGERIA

□ Ijeshaland

SOUTH AFRICA

□ Alexandra
(affiliated project)

Durban □

TANZANIA

□ Kasulu

UGANDA

□ Gulu
(Temporarily suspended due to
political disturbance)

□ Kasese

ZAMBIA

Chanyanya □

ZAIRE

□ Gemena

□ Basankusu

Ntondo □ Mbandaka
□ Lake Tumba Expansion
Baraka □

□ Kinshasa
□ Kikwit
Kingabwa

177

ASIA/PACIFIC REGION

INDIA

INDONESIA

PAKISTAN

PAPUA NEW GUINEA

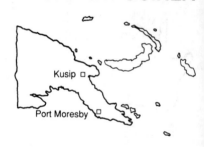

PHILIPPINES

SOLOMON ISLANDS

NORTH AMERICAN NATIONAL/REGIONAL CENTERS

Habitat Canada West

Habitat Canada Central

Habitat Canada
Maritime Provinces

Habitat Midwest

Habitat Northeast

Habitat West
(includes Hawaii and Alaska)

Rocky Mountain Habitat

Habitat Heartland

Habitat Mideast

Habitat Mid-Atlantic

Habitat South Atlantic

Habitat Southwest

Habitat South

Habitat Southeast

★ - REGIONAL CENTER
✳ - NATIONAL/REGIONAL CENTER

AUSTRALIA

Adelaide

Sydney
Wollongong

Melbourne

*Affiliated Project

Maps shown are not to scale.

REGIONAL AND NATIONAL CENTERS

Habitat Australia
Ted Swisher
Unit 4/40 Carrington Road
Castle Hill 2154
AUSTRALIA
(011) 612-899-4409
FAX: (011) 612-634-2867

Habitat Canada
Maritime Provinces
Regional Director:
Louise McNeil
23 Argyle Street
Sydney, Cape Breton
Nova Scotia, B1S 2T8 CANADA
902-564-0731

Eastern Ontario
Quebec
Regional Director:
Mary Dodge
125 Brentcliffe Road
Toronto, Ontario M4G 3Y7
CANADA
416-429-4748

Western Ontario
Manitoba
Western Provinces
Regional Director:
Jake Pauls
181 Church Avenue
Winnipeg, Manitoba R2W 1B6
CANADA
204-589-5371

Habitat Heartland
Arkansas
Kansas
Missouri
Nebraska
Regional Director:
Carolyn Talboys
P.O. Box 8955
Springfield, MO 65801-8955
417-831-0982

Habitat Mid-Atlantic
Delaware
Maryland
Southern New Jersey
Pennsylvania
Northern Virginia
Washington, DC
West Virginia
Regional Director:
Jim Tyree
P.O. Box 6860
1829 North 19th Street
Philadelphia, PA 19132
215-765-8303

Habitat Mideast
Indiana
Kentucky
Ohio
Regional Directors:
Hubert and Fran Ping
Route 1, Box 86A
Thorntown, IN 46071
317-325-2516

Habitat Midwest
Illinois
Iowa
Michigan
Minnesota
North Dakota
South Dakota
Wisconsin
Regional Director:
Bill Ward
6601 South Central
Bedford Park, IL 60638-6399
708-496-0909
FAX: 708-458-8992

Habitat Northeast
Connecticut
Maine
Massachusetts
New Hampshire
Northern New Jersey
New York
Rhode Island
Vermont
Regional Director:
Barbara Yates
Associate Regional Dir.:
Rick Moore
P.O. Box 322
Acton, MA 01720
508-264-0353

Habitat South
Alabama
Louisiana
Mississippi
Central Tennessee
Western Tennessee
Regional Director:
Luther Millsaps
P.O. Box 854
Tupelo, MS 38802
601-844-2397

Habitat South Atlantic
North Carolina
South Carolina
Eastern Tennessee
Southern Virginia
Regional Director:
Sandra Graham
Associate Regional Dir.:
Gilbert Edson
P.O. Box 624
Easley, SC 29640
803-855-1102

Habitat Southeast
Florida
Georgia
Regional Director:
Jerry Kalish
Habitat and Church Streets
Americus, GA 31709-3423
912-924-6935

Habitat Southwest
Oklahoma
Texas
Regional Director:
Joe Gatlin
P.O. Box 3005
Waco, TX 76707
817-756-7575
Associate Regional Dir.:
Keith Branson
4921 Jean Street
Corpus Christi, TX 78411
512-854-4416

Habitat West (northern office)
Alaska
Northern California
Northern Nevada
Oregon
Washington
Regional Director:
Sally Evers
890 Morse Avenue
Sacramento, CA 95864
916-489-7628

Habitat West (southern office)
Southern California
Southern Nevada
Arizona
Hawaii
Regional Director:
Ken Karlstad
19961 Gray Lane
Orange, CA 92669
714-532-3982

Rocky Mountain Habitat
Colorado
Idaho
Montana
New Mexico
Utah
Wyoming
Regional Director:
Ray Finney
913 East Ninth Avenue
Denver, CO 80218
303-832-4208

AFFILIATED PROJECTS

Alabama
  Greater Birmingham HFH
  Lee County HFH (Auburn)
  HFH in Mobile County (Mobile)
  Montevallo Area HFH
  Montgomery HFH
  North Alabama HFH, Inc.
    (Huntsville)
  Habitat Selma!, Inc.
  Shoals HFH, Inc. (Florence)
  Habitat Tuscaloosa, Inc.

Arizona
  Maricopa HFH (Sun City)
  Tucson HFH
  HFH Valley of the Sun
    (Phoenix)

Arkansas
  Arkansas Valley HFH
    (Ft. Smith)
  El Dorado HFH
  HFH of Pulaski County
    (Little Rock)
California
  Bay & Valley HFH, Inc.
    (San Jose)
  HFH Coachella Valley
    (Indio)
  East Bay HFH, Inc. (Oakland)
  Foothills HFH, Inc. (Auburn)
  HFH Fresno, Inc.
  Humboldt HFH, Inc. (Eureka)
  HFH of Orange Country, Inc.
    (Orange)

Peninsula HFH (Redwood City)
HFH Riverside, Inc.
Sacramento HFH, Inc.
HFH/Santa Cruz County
    (Santa Cruz)
Siskiyou HFH, Inc. (Weed)
HFH of Sonoma County
    (Santa Rosa)
Tijuana-San Diego HFH
HFH of Ventura

Colorado
Denver HFH
Greeley Area HFH, Inc.
Larimer County HFH
    (Loveland)
Pikes Peak HFH, Inc.
    (Colorado Springs)
HFH of the St. Vrain Valley
    (Longmont)

Connecticut
HFH of Greater Bridgeport,
    Connecticut
Hartford Area HFH
HFH-New Haven, Inc.
HFH of Southeastern
    Connecticut (New London)

Delaware
HFH of New Castle County,
    Inc. (Wilmington)
District of Columbia
D.C. HFH (Washington, D.C.)

Florida
Alachua HFH (Gainesville)
HFH of Broward, Inc.
    (Oakland Park)
Charlotte County HFH
    (Port Charlotte)
Clay County HFH
    (Penney Farms)

Halifax HFH, Inc.
    (Ormond Beach)
Immokalee HFH
Jackson Country HFH, Inc.
    (Marianna)
HFH of Jacksonville
HFH of Lake County, Florida,
    Inc. (Fruitland Park)
Lee County HFH (Ft. Myers)
HFH Manasota, Inc.
    (Sarasota)
Martin/St. Lucie HFH (Stuart)
HFH of Greater Miami, Inc.
HFH of Greater Orlando Area
HFH of Palm Beach County
    (West Palm Beach)
Pensacola HFH
Pinellas HFH (St. Petersburg)
South Brevard HFH, Inc.
    (Melbourne)
Southeast Volusia HFH, Inc.
    (New Smyrna Beach)
Space Coast HFH, Inc.
    (Titusville)
Tallahassee HFH
Tampa Habitat
HFH of the Upper Keys, Inc.
    (Key Largo)
West Volusia HFH (Deland)
Winter Haven HFH, Inc.

Georgia
HFH/Albany Area
Americus HFH
Athens Area HFH
Atlanta HFH
Augusta/CSRA HFH
Bainbridge-Decatur County
    HFH, Inc.
Cartersville-Bartow County
    HFH

Cherokee County HFH
  (Acworth)
HFH Clayton County, Georgia,
  Inc. (Jonesboro)
Coastal Empire HFH
  (Savannah)
Cobb County HFH (Marietta)
Columbus Area HFH
Dalton HFH
HFH-DeKalb, Inc. (Decatur)
HFH/Glynn County
  (Brunswick)
Griffin Area HFH, Inc.
Gwinnett County HFH
  (Norcross)
HFH of Hall County, Inc.
  (Gainesville)
Henry County HFH
  (McDonough)
Lee County HFH, Inc.
  (Leesburg)
Macon Area HFH
Monroe County HFH (Forsyth)
Newton-Morgan Area HFH
  (Oxford)
North Central Georgia HFH
  (Ellijay)
HFH of Northeast Georgia, Inc.
  (Demorest)
Peach Area HFH (Ft. Valley)
HFH of Rabun County
  (Clayton)
HFH of Rome and Floyd
  County
Thomasville-Thomas County
  Habitat
The Georgia Tri-County HFH,
  Inc. (Talbotton)
Valdosta-Lowndes County
  HFH
West Georgia HFH (Carrollton)

Hawaii
Hawaii HFH (Honolulu)

Idaho
HFH/North Idaho
  (Coeur d'Alene)

Illinois
Albany Park/HFH (Chicago)
Chicago South Region HFH
  (Chicago Heights)
HFH of Danville, Inc.
Decatur Area HFH
East St. Louis HFH
HFH/Lake County, Illinois
  (Waukegan)
Logos HFH, Inc. (Cairo)
HFH of McLean County
  (Bloomington)
Pembroke HFH (St. Anne)
HFH/Greater Peoria Area
Pilsen/Little Village HFH
  (Chicago)
Rockford Area HFH, Inc.
HFH/Sangamon County
Uptown HFH (Chicago)
Westside HFH (Chicago)
Will County HFH (Joliet)

Indiana
HFH of Boone County
  (Lebanon)
HFH of Elkhart County
  (Goshen)
HFH of Evansville
Fort Wayne HFH
Huntington County HFH
  (Huntington)
HFH of Greater Indianapolis
HFH of the Kokomo
  Community
La Porte County HFH, Inc.
  (La Porte)

HFH of Lafayette
Madison County HFH
(Anderson)
HFH of Monroe County
(Bloomington)
Greater Muncie, Indiana HFH
Noble County HFH (Ligonier)
Northwest Indiana HFH
(Hammond)
Putnam County HFH, Inc.
(Greencastle)
HFH of St. Joseph County, Inc.
(Notre Dame)
Wabash Valley HFH, Inc.
(Terre Haute)

Iowa
Cedar Valley HFH
(Cedar Rapids)
Des Moines HFH:
S.H.E.L.T.E.R.

Kansas
Kaw Valley HFH, Inc.
(Kansas City)
Lawrence HFH
Topeka HFH
Wichita HFH

Kentucky
Ashland-Ironton Area HFH
(Ashland)
Lexington HFH, Inc.
HFH of Metro Louisville
Marshall County HFH, Inc.
(Benton)
Morehead Area HFH
Murray-Calloway County HFH
Northern Kentucky HFH
(Newport)
HFH of Owensboro/Daviess
County

Paducah HFH
Woodford County HFH, Inc.
(Versailles)

Louisiana
HFH of Greater Baton Rouge
Covington HFH
New Orleans Area HFH
North Central Louisiana HFH
(Ruston)
Rapides HFH (Alexandria)
Washington HFH (Bogalusa)

Maine
Androscoggin HFH (Greene)
HFH of Greater Bangor
Hancock County HFH
(Ellsworth)
HFH/Greater Portland, Inc.
Habitat York County, Inc.
(Ogunquit)

Maryland
Arundel HFH, Inc.
(Severna Park)
HFH in Charles County, MD
(La Plata)
Chesapeake HFH (Baltimore)
Garrett County HFH, Inc.
(Oakland)
Habitat on Maryland's Lower
Shore (Salisbury)
Montgomery County, Maryland
HFH (Rockville)
HFH, Prince George's County
(Greenbelt)
Sandtown HFH (Baltimore)

Massachusetts
Attleboro Area HFH
(North Attleboro)
Habitat Boston (Dorchester)
HFH of Cape Cod (Brewster)

185

Greater Lawrence HFH
(Andover)
Lynn HFH
North Worcester County HFH
(Leominster)
Pioneer Valley HFH (Amherst)
South Shore HFH (Norwell)
Greater Springfield HFH
(Ludlow)
Habitat Worcester, Inc.

Michigan

HFH Alpena Area
HFH/Barry County (Middleville)
Battle Creek Area HFH
Gladwin County HFH
(Beaverton)
Grand Rapids HFH, Inc.
HFH Grand Traverse Region
(Traverse City)
HFH/Huron Valley (Ann Arbor)
HFH of Isabella County
(Mt. Pleasant)
Greater Jackson HFH, Inc.
Kalamazoo Valley HFH
Lake County HFH (Baldwin)
HFH/Lansing (East Lansing)
HFH/Lenawee County (Adrian)
HFH Metro Detroit
Midland County HFH
Muskegon County
Cooperating Churches HFH
(Muskegon)
HFH of Niles-Buchanan Area,
Inc.
HFH/Portland (Lyons)
Saginaw HFH
South Haven Area HFH
Tri-Cities Area HFH (Grand
Haven)
Wexford HFH (Cadillac)

Minnesota

HFH-Duluth
St. Cloud Area HFH
Twin Cities HFH, Inc.
(Minneapolis)

Mississippi

Bolivar County HFH
(Cleveland)
Clarksdale Area HFH, Inc.
Clinton HFH
Coahoma HFH, Inc.
Columbus-Lowndes HFH
(Columbus)
Greenwood-Leflore HFH, Inc.
(Greenwood)
Harrison County HFH (Gulfport)
Holmes County HFH
(Lexington)
Kosciusko-Attala HFH
(Kosciusko)
Lauderdale County HFH
(Meridian)
HFH/Metro Jackson
Northeast Mississippi HFH
(Tupelo)
Oxford-Lafayette County
Habitat, Inc.
Panola Habitat (Batesville)
Starkville HFH
HFH of Sunflower County
(Doddsville)
Union County HFH, Inc. (New
Albany)
Washington County HFH
(Greenville)
West Tallahatchie HFH
(Sumner)

Missouri

Barton County HFH, Inc.
(Lamar)

HFH-Cape Area (Cape
  Girardeau)
City and County HFH
  (St. Louis)
Joplin Area HFH
Kansas City HFH
Mountain Country HFH
  (Branson)
Northwest Missouri HFH, Inc.
  (St. Joseph)
HFH, Odessa R-VII Area, Inc.
  (Odessa)
Sedalia Area HFH, Inc.
Show Me Central HFH
  (Columbia)
HFH of Springfield, Missouri,
  Inc.

Montana
HFH of Flathead Valley
  (Kalispell)

Nebraska
Lincoln HFH, Inc.
Omaha HFH, Inc.

New Hampshire
Cheshire County HFH (Keene)
HFH of the Kearsarge/Sunapee
  Area (New London)
Lakes Region HFH (Laconia)
Merrimack HFH (Penacook)
Ossipee Mountains HFH
  (Wolfeboro Falls)
Pemi-Valley Habitat (Ashland)

New Jersey
Burlington County HFH
  (Mt. Holly)
Metropolitan Camden HFH
  (Gloucester City)
Cumberland County HFH, Inc.
  (Bridgeton)

Freehold Area HFH (Freehold)
Gloucester County HFH
  (Pitman)
Morris HFH (Morristown)
HFH/Newark, New Jersey
Paterson HFH
Greater Plainfield HFH
  (Watchung)
Salem County HFH (Elmer)
HFH-Trenton Area (Princeton)

New Mexico
Greater Albuquerque HFH
Deming HFH
HFH/Gila Region
  (Silver City)
Mesilla Valley HFH
  (Las Cruces)
Santa Fe HFH

New York
HFH-Brooklyn, New York
HFH/Buffalo
Capital District HFH (Albany)
Cazenovia Area HFH
Chautauqua Area HFH
  (Jamestown)
Chemung County HFH (Elmira)
Flower City HFH (Rochester)
Genesee Valley HFH
  (Houghton)
Hamilton HFH
Mid-Hudson Valley HFH, Inc.
  (Poughkeepsie)
HFH New York City, Inc.,
  (Lower East Side)
North Country HFH (Malone)
Northern Susquehanna Valley
  HFH (Oneonta)
Raquette Valley HFH (Norfolk)
HFH of Suffolk, Inc.
  (East Setauket)

Syracuse HFH, Inc.
Tioga HFH (Owego)
Groton Tri-County HFH, Inc.
  (Groton)
HFH of Wayne County, New
  York, Inc. (Macedon)
HFH of Westchester County
  (Valhalla)

North Carolina
HFH of Alamance County,
  N.C., Inc. (Burlington)
Blue Ridge HFH (Boone)
HFH of Burke County, Inc.
  (Morganton)
HFH/Cabarrus County
  (Concord)
Cape Fear HFH, Inc.
  (Wilmington)
Carteret County HFH
  (Morehead City)
HFH of Catawba Valley
  (Hickory)
HFH of Charlotte, Inc.
Chatham County HFH
  (Pittsboro)
HFH in Cleveland County
  (Shelby)
Davidson HFH
Durham County HFH (Durham)
Fayetteville Area HFH, Inc.
  (Hope Mills)
HFH of Forsyth County, Inc.
  (Winston-Salem)
Franklin County HFH
  (Louisburg)
HFH of Gastonia
HFH of Greater Goldsboro
HFH of Greater Greensboro,
  Inc.
Halifax/Northampton HFH, Inc.
  (Roanoke Rapids)

Henderson County HFH
  (Hendersonville)
Hertford County HFH
  (Ahoskie)
HFH of High Point
HFH of the Lexington, NC
  Area, Inc.
Madison County HFH
  (Marshall)
HFH of Matthews, Inc.
McDowell County HFH
  (Marion)
HFH of Moore County, Inc.
  (Southern Pines)
HFH of Greater New Bern, Inc.
Orange County Habitat
  (Chapel Hill)
Greater Reidsville HFH
Rutherford County HFH
  (Rutherfordton)
HFH Sanford, Inc.
Stanly County HFH
  (Albemarle)
Statesville-Iredell HFH
  (Statesville)
Thermal Belt HFH (Tryon)
HFH of Thomasville Area, Inc.
Transylvania HFH, Inc.
  (Brevard)
Upper Yadkin Valley HFH
  (Elkin)
HFH of Wake County (Raleigh)
Western North Carolina HFH
  (Asheville)

North Dakota
Red River Valley HFH
  (Grand Forks)

Ohio
HFH of Greater Akron, Inc.
HFH of Greater Canton, Inc.

Cincinnati HFH
Clermont County HFH (Milford)
Greater Cleveland HFH
Greater Columbus HFH
Dayton, Ohio HFH
Firelands HFH (Huron)
HFH-Hamilton! (Hamilton)
Interchurch HFH of Knox
County (Mt. Vernon)
Licking County HFH (Granville)
Lorain County HFH (Oberlin)
Maumee Valley HFH (Toledo)
Millcreek Valley HFH
(Cincinnati)
HFH of Portage County
(Ravenna)
Richland County HFH
(Mansfield)
Sandusky County HFH
(Fremont)
Seneca HFH, Inc. (Tiffin)
HFH Greater Steubenville Area
HFH within Trumbull County
(Niles)
Wayne County HFH (Wooster)
Zanesville HFH

Oklahoma
Bartlesville Area HFH, Inc.
Central Oklahoma HFH
(Oklahoma City)
Enid HFH
Tulsa Metropolitan Area HFH,
Inc.

Oregon
Bend Area HFH
HFH/Mt. Angel Area, Inc.
Portland HFH
HFH/Rogue Valley (Medford)
Willamette West HFH, Inc.
(Portland)

Pennsylvania
Adams County Chapter HFH
(Gettysburg)
HFH in Bloomsburg
HFH of Butler County, Inc.
(Butler)
HFH of Chester County
(West Chester)
Greater Erie Area HFH
Greene County HFH
(Waynesburg)
HFH in Harrisburg
Huntingdon Area HFH
Lancaster Area HFH
HFH of the Lehigh Valley
(Bethlehem)
Norristown HFH, Inc.
HFH North Central
Philadelphia
HFH West Philadelphia
Pittsburgh HFH
Reading/Berks HFH (Reading)
Tri-County Pennsylvania HFH
(State College)
Washington County HFH
York HFH, Inc.

Rhode Island
HFH-Rhode Island
(Providence)

South Carolina
Aiken County HFH, Inc. (Aiken)
Anderson County HFH
(Anderson)
Central South Carolina HFH
(Columbia)
Charleston HFH
Colleton HFH (Walterboro)
Greenville County HFH
(Greenville)
Greenwood Area HFH

189

Hampton HFH
Oconee HFH (Westminster)
Pickens HFH (Clemson)
Sea Island HFH (Johns Island)
HFH of Spartanburg
Sumter HFH
HFH of York County, South
    Carolina, Inc. (Rock Hill)

South Dakota
HFH of Greater Sioux Falls

Tennessee
Appalachia HFH (Robbins)
HFH of Greater Chattanooga,
    Inc.
Holston HFH (Kingsport)
Jackson Area HFH
Knoxville HFH
Maury County HFH (Columbia)
HFH-Mid-South, Inc.
    (Memphis)
Nashville Area HFH
Rutherford County Area HFH
    (Murfreesboro)

Texas
Amarillo HFH
Austin HFH, Inc.
Beaumont HFH
Bryan-College Station HFH
    (Bryan)
HFH/Corpus Christi
Dallas HFH
HFH of El Paso
Fort Worth Area HFH
Greenville, Texas HFH
HFH-Northwest Harris County
    (Spring)
Houston HFH, Inc.
Kerr County HFH (Kerrville)
Longview HFH
Lubbock HFH

Montgomery County HFH
    (Conroe)
Rio Grande HFH (McAllen)
San Antonio HFH
HFH of Smith County (Tyler)
HFH of Texarkana
Waco HFH
Walker County HFH
    (Huntsville)

Utah
HFH/Northern Utah
    (Brigham City)
Salt Lake Valley HFH
    (Salt Lake City)

Vermont
Brattleboro Area HFH
Central Vermont HFH
    (E. Montpelier)
Green Mountain HFH
    (Williston)
Northeast Kingdom HFH
    (Greensboro)
Rutland Region HFH, Inc.
Upper Valley HFH (Quechee)

Virginia
Central Valley HFH, Inc.
    (Bridgewater)
Eastern Shore of Virginia HFH,
    Inc. (Keller)
Greater Lynchburg HFH
HFH of Martinsville and Henry
    County
New River Valley HFH
    (Christiansburg)
Peninsula HFH (Newport News)
Richmond Metropolitan HFH,
    Inc.
HFH in the Roanoke Valley
    (Roanoke)

Rockbridge Area HFH
(Lexington)
South Hampton Roads HFH
(Portsmouth)

Washington
Cowlitz County HFH
(Longview)
Seattle HFH
Snoqualmie Valley HFH
(Carnation)
South Puget Sound HFH
(Olympia)
Spokane HFH
Tacoma/Pierce County HFH
HFH in Whatcom County
(Lynden)
Yakima Valley Partners/HFH
(Buena)

West Virginia
Almost Heaven HFH
(Circleville)
Mountaineer HFH, Inc.
(Charleston)
HFH of Pocahontas County,
Inc. (Marlinton)
Preston County HFH, Inc.
(Kingwood)

Wisconsin
Central Wisconsin HFH, Inc.
(Stevens Point)
Milwaukee HFH
Northeast Wisconsin HFH
(Green Bay)

HFH of Oregon/Brooklyn
(Oregon)
Portage Area HFH, Inc.
Racine HFH, Inc.
Southwest Wisconsin HFH
(Dodgeville)
Two Rivers-Manitowoc HFH
(Two Rivers)
HFH/Waukesha County
(Waukesha)

Canada
Ontario
Oakville HFH
Owen Sound HFH
(Sauble Beach)
HFH-Toronto
HFH-Waterloo Region
(St. Jacobs)
Manitoba
Winkler HFH
Winnipeg, Manitoba HFH

Australia
Adelaide HFH
HFH New South Wales (Castle
Hill)
HFH Victoria (Hawthorn)
Wollongong HFH (Wollongong,
New South Wales)

South Africa
Alexandra HFH

Appendix C

Habitat for Humanity
Campus Chapters
Alphabetical listing by state
(as of April 1, 1990)

Alabama
- The University of Alabama (Tuscaloosa)
- Auburn University
- Birmingham-Southern College

California
- Azusa Pacific University
- California State University-Fresno
- University of California-Irvine
- University of California-San Diego
- University of California-Santa Cruz
- Pepperdine University (Malibu)
- Santa Clara University
- Westmont College (Santa Barbara)

Connecticut
- The Hotchkiss School (Lakeville)

District of Columbia
- American University
- The Catholic University of America

Florida
- Bethune-Cookman College (Daytona Beach)
- Eckerd College (St. Pertersburg)
- University of Florida (Gainesville)
- Jesuit High School (Tampa)
- Palm Beach Community College
- Stetson University (Deland)

Georgia
Berry College (Rome)
Emory University (Atlanta)
Fort Valley State College
Georgia State University (Atlanta)
Georgia Southern College (Statesboro)
Marist School (Atlanta)

Illinois
Bradley University (Peoria)
Eureka College
North Park College (Chicago)

Indiana
Ball State University (Muncie)
DePauw University (Greencastle)
Earlham College (Richmond)
Goshen College
Manchester College (North Manchester)
University of Notre Dame
Purdue University (West Lafayette)
Saint Joseph's College (Rensselaer)

Iowa
Iowa State University (Ames)
Simpson College (Indianola)

Kentucky
Asbury Theological Seminary (Wilmore)
Centre College (Danville)
University of Kentucky (Lexington)

Maryland
Hood College (Frederick)

Massachusetts
Massachusetts Institute of Technology (Cambridge)
Mount Greylock Regional High School (Williamstown)
Tufts University (Medford)

Michigan
Calvin College (Grand Rapids)
Kalamazoo College
Western Michigan University (Kalamazoo)

Minnesota
Bethel College and Seminary (St. Paul)

Mississippi
Millsaps College (Jackson)
Mississippi State University (Starkville)
University of Mississippi (Oxford)

Missouri
William Jewell College (Liberty)

New Jersey
Montclair State College (Upper Montclair)

New York
Bronx Community College
Cornell University (Ithaca)
Houghton College
Ithaca College

North Carolina
Duke University (Durham)
Elon College
High Point College
University of North Carolina—Chapel Hill
University of North Carolina—Greensboro
North Carolina State University (Raleigh)
Northern High School (Durham)
Wake Forest University (Winston-Salem)

Ohio
University of Akron
Bluffton College
University of Dayton
Denison University (Granville)
Malone College (Canton)
Miami University (Oxford)
Ohio Wesleyan University (Delaware)
Walsh College (Canton)
Wittenberg University (Springfield)
The College of Wooster

Oklahoma
    Northeastern State University (Tahlequah)
    Oklahoma State University (Stillwater)

Oregon
    Linfield College (McMinnville)

Pennsylvania
    Allegheny College (Meadville)
    Bloomsburg College
    Dickinson College (Carlisle)
    Eastern College (St. Davids)
    Elizabethtown College
    Franklin and Marshall College (Lancaster)
    Geneva College (Beaver Falls)
    Gettysburg College
    Gwynedd-Mercy College (Gwynedd Valley)
    Lehigh University (Bethlehem)
    Penn State University (University Park)
    Saint Joseph's University (Philadelphia)
    Susquehanna University (Selinsgrove)
    Villanova University
    Westminster College (New Wilmington)

South Carolina
    Erskine College (Due West)
    Furman University (Greenville)
    Presbyterian College (Clinton)
    Spartanburg Colleges and Universities

South Dakota
    Augustana College (Sioux Falls)

Tennessee
    Rhodes College (Memphis)

Texas
    Baylor University (Waco)
    Dallas Baptist University
    East Texas State University (Commerce)
    Texas A&M University (College Station)
    University of Texas—Austin
    Texas Christian University (Fort Worth)

Virginia
Lynchburg College
University of Richmond
Virginia Polytechnic Institute and State University (Blacksburg)
Virginia Wesleyan College (Norfolk)

Washington
Western Washington University (Bellingham)
Whitworth College (Spokane)

Wisconsin
Carroll College (Waukesha)

Appendix D

Habitat for Humanity International Headquarters Staff Roster
(as of April 1, 1990)

Executive
- Millard Fuller, Director
- Linda Fuller, Assistant
- Paul Davis and Julie Peeples, Chaplains

Administrative
- Karen Higgs, Director
- Clydia Duhon, Supervisor, Shipping and Receiving
- Michael Edge, Supervisor, Accounting Operations
- Mark Lassman-Eul, Associate Director, Personnel
- Bonnie Little, Administrative Assistant
- David Macfarlane, Director, Computer Services
- Amy Parsons, Supervisor, Recruiting
- Paul Phillips, Supervisor, Reporting and Analysis
- Miles Richmond, Supervisor, Purchasing and Inventory Control
- Diane and Jody Umstead, Childcare Coordinators
- George Walton, Director, Personnel
- Daniel Wise, Director, Finance

Development
- Carol Pezzelli Wise, Director
- Craig Bunyea, Art Director
- Bill Burnett, Associate Director
- Joan Burnett, Director, Vision Habitat
- Gene Crumley, Associate Director
- Mamie Dunston, Director of Donor Management
- Darryl McMillan, Director of Public Relations
- Jim Purks, Senior Writer
- Clive Rainey, Senior Associate

Doralee Robertson, Director of Media
Jeff Snider, Grant Writer
Kim Wilson, Associate Director

Operations
David Rowe, Director
  Affiliate Operations
    Rick Hathaway, Director
    Steve Baker, Director, Habitat for Homeless Humanity
    Lynn Baugh, Maintenance Coordinator
    Peter Beard, Staff Counsel
    Linda Carl, Director, Habitat for Humanity with Disabilities
    Martin Fox, Construction Resources Coordinator
    Carol Gregory, Director, Affiliate Programs
    Tom Hall, Director, Workshops and Affiliate Training
    Walter Money, Construction Supervisor
    Al Newkirk, Construction Supervisor
    Hattie Pitts, Americus Project Homeowner Assistant
    Samuel Reist, Director, Americus Construction
    Johnny Roberts, Construction Supervisor
    Mark Simmons, Construction Supervisor
    Claire Williams, Associate Director
    Robert O. Wilson, Director, Jimmy Carter Work Projects
  Campus Chapters
    David McDaniels, Director
    Jane McDaniels, Assistant
  International Operations
    Sam Bandela, Asia Coordinator
    Robert Dunsmore, Latin America Coordinator
    Margaret Harvey, Director, Global Village Program
    Gary Manzo, Trainer
    Frank Purvis, Appropriate Technology Coordinator
    Robert Reid, Pacific Coordinator
    Susan Rhema, Director, International Training
    Dan Roman, Field Office Director, Zaire
    Winston Slider, East and South Africa Coordinator
    Scott Smith, Trainer
    Mary Margaret Velasquez-Bertram, Latin America Coordinator
    John Yeatman, West and Central Africa Coordinator
  Minority Partnership Development
    Kathyie Doyle, Director

Appendix E

Habitat for Humanity International, Inc.
Board of Directors and Advisors
(as of April 1, 1990)

Board of Directors

Geoffrey Van Loucks (President)
Los Gatos, CA
United Church of Christ
Murray Branch, Atlanta, GA
Progressive National Baptist
Norma Caluscusan, Dumaguete
City, PHILIPPINES
Assembly of God
Anthony Campolo, St. Davids, PA
American Baptist
Margaret Chrisman, Paradise
Valley, AZ
Presbyterian
Gary Cook, Dallas, TX
Southern Baptist
Javier Elizondo, Franklin, TN
Southern Baptist
Louis Fischer, Wayne, PA
Roman Catholic
P.V. George, Syracuse, NY
United Church of Christ
Martha Graham, Brooklyn, NY
Roman Catholic
Frank Lennon, Cohasset, MA
Church of God in Christ
Mary McCahon, Bayside, NY
United Church of Christ

Gerard Mpango, Kasulu,
TANZANIA
Anglican
Zenon Colque Rojas, Arequipa,
PERU
Roman Catholic
Warren Sawyer, Swampscott, MA
United Church of Christ
Cynthia Sayre, Frankfort, KY
Disciples of Christ
Mary Elizabeth Schumacher,
(Vice-President) Boulder, CO
Episcopalian
Edgar Stoesz, Akron, PA
Mennonite
Larry Stoner, Lititz, PA
Mennonite
Jack Takayanagi (Secretary)
Portland, OR
United Church of Christ
Robert Thompson, Toronto,
Ontario, CANADA
United Church of Canada
Clyde Tilley (Treasurer)
Jackson, TN
Southern Baptist
LeRoy Troyer, Mishawaka, IN
Mennonite

Mel West, Columbia, MO
United Methodist
John Wieland, Atlanta, GA
Presbyterian
Earl Wilson, Indianapolis, IN
United Church of Christ
Andrew Young, Atlanta, GA
United Church of Christ

Board of Advisors

Franklin C. Basler (Coordinator)
Tryon, NC
United Church of Christ
Kerry Abbott, East Jerusalem,
ISRAEL
Episcopalian
Chris Alghini, Wooster, OH
Roman Catholic
George Anderson, Palm Harbor,
FL
United Church of Canada
Gordon Archibald, Hampton, NH
Congregational
Harold Auler, Jr., Asheboro, NC
United Church of Christ
John Austin, Marissa, IL
United Church of Christ
Ellen Baer, Armonk, NY
United Methodist
Frank T. Baker, Elderton, PA
Lutheran
Thomas Baker, Rex, GA
Southern Baptist
Jacob Battle, Leslie, GA
Nondenominational
Fred Bauman, Zillah, WA
Mennonite
John Bell, Winston-Salem, NC
Presbyterian
Cliff Bellar, Akron, OH
United Church of Christ

Robert Bennett, Albany, GA
Unitarian-Universalist
Kenneth Bensen, Lansing, MI
United Methodist
Pam Bolles, Clarksburg, MO
United Methodist
Landrum Bolling, Washington, DC
Society of Friends
John Bontreger, Indianapolis, IN
Mennonite
Dawn Boulanger, Toronto,
Ontario, CANADA
Episcopalian
Robert Bratcher, Chapel Hill, NC
Southern Baptist
Martin Brooks, Vestal, NY
United Methodist
Allen & Sharon Brown, Farmland,
IN
United Church of Christ
Joseph Buckwalter, Chapel Hill,
NC
American Baptist/Southern
Baptist
Ed Carlson, Rockford, IL
Salvation Army
Floyd Carmack, Jonesboro, GA
United Church of Christ
James B. Carr, Baldwinsville, NY
United Church of Christ
Jim Carr, Clarendon Hills, IL
Evangelical Covenant
Rosalynn Carter, Plains, GA
Southern Baptist
Howard Caskey, Southampton,
PA
United Methodist
Chuck Clark, Atlanta, GA
Nondenominational
Pat Clark, Montgomery, AL
American Baptist

Bill Clarke, Canton, OH
Presbyterian
Wayne K. Clymer, Wayzata,
MN
United Methodist
Orville Coats, Rocklin, CA
United Methodist
Eugene Coffin, Desert Hot
Springs, CA
Society of Friends
Frances Jones Collier, Key Largo,
FL
Episcopalian
Thomas Connell, Tryon, NC
Presbyterian
Margaret Cook, Westwood, NJ
United Church of Christ
John Crosland, Charlotte, NC
Presbyterian
Dale Cross, Clarkston, GA
Southern Baptist
John F. Dallas, Augusta, GA
United Methodist
Ernest (Jeff) Davis, Plymouth, NH
United Church of Christ
Arthur DeFehr, Winnipeg,
Manitoba, CANADA
Mennonite/Brethren
Sue DeJournett, Americus, GA
United Methodist
Randall Dew, Paducah, KY
United Methodist
Emily Diamond, Covington, LA
Nondenominational
Chitty Dominado, Dumaguete
City, PHILIPPINES
Roman Catholic
Robert John Doran, Albany, NY
Ecumenical
John Dorean, Jefferson, PA
American Baptist

David Dorsey, Richmond, VA
Baptist
Rolland Dutton, Winter Haven, FL
Southern Baptist
Thomas East, Jr., Tupelo, MS
United Methodist
David L. Eastis, Los Gatos, CA
Presbyterian
David M. Eastis, Los Gatos, CA
United Church of Christ
Sam Emerick, Port Charlotte, FL
United Methodist
David Ewing, Americus, GA
Southern Baptist
Richard & Georgene Fabian,
Holderness, NH
United Church of Christ
Ron J. Foust, Americus, GA
Roman Catholic
Roger Fredrickson, Sioux Falls,
SD
American Baptist
Mark Frey, Indianapolis, IN
United Church of Christ
Robert & Myrna Gemmer, St.
Petersburg, FL
Church of the Brethren
Robert Gerdes, Salt Lake City, UT
Presbyterian
Andrew Gibson, Midland, MI
United Church of Christ
Rachel & Everett Gill, Stone
Mountain, GA
Southern Baptist
Amy Grant, Nashville, TN
Transdenominational
Gertrude Green, Savannah, GA
Episcopalian
Jay & Lisa Guffey, Springfield,
MO
United Methodist

Bruce C. Gunter, Atlanta, GA
Episcopalian
Keith Harris, Richmond, VA
Southern Baptist
Daryl & Kay Hartzler, Lake
Odessa, MI
United Methodist
Kenneth M. Henson, Jr.,
Columbus, GA
United Methodist
Norman F. Heyl, Crofton, MD
Presbyterian
Eric Hines, Durham, NC
Southern Baptist
Tim Holtz, Richmond, VA
Southern Baptist
Walden & Alice Howard,
Salisbury, MD
Presbyterian
Romando James, Clemson, SC
Assembly of God
Keith Jaspers, Springfield, MO
United Methodist
Lynwood B. Jenkins, Mineral,
VA
Presbyterian
Patricia Johnson, Baconton, GA
Baptist
Helen Kennedy, Lamar, IN
United Church of Christ
Loree Kirk, Waterford, MI
United Church of Christ
Jonathan Knight, Syracuse, NY
Presbyterian
Arnold "Skip" Larson,
Chesterfield, MO
United Church of Christ
Bruce Larson, Seattle, WA
Presbyterian
Paul LaRue, Dallas, OR
United Methodist

Karen Lassman-Eul, Americus,
GA
Mennonite
Harleyn Lee, Germantown, IN
United Methodist
Ann Little, Louisville, KY
Lutheran
Ralph Loew, Buffalo, NY
Lutheran
Randall & Lou Lolley, Wake
Forest, NC
Southern Baptist
Armando Jesus Lopez, Oxnard,
CA
Roman Catholic
Sam Lott, Americus, GA
United Methodist
Faith Lytle, San Antonio, TX
Presbyterian
Ken MacHarg, Louisville, KY
United Church of Christ
Avery C. Manchester, Greenwich,
CT
United Methodist
Beth Marcus, Holland, MI
Reformed Church
Carolyn Anne Martin, Statesboro,
GA
Presbyterian
J. David Matthews,
Winston-Salem, NC
Southern Baptist
Robert Mayo, West Granby, CT
United Methodist
Don McClanen, Germantown,
MD
Ecumenical
Delores McMillin, Evansville, IN
Presbyterian
Joyce Millen, Akron, PA
Mennonite

Robert Miller, East Cleveland, OH
Presbyterian
Roger Miller, Woodland, CA
United Church of Christ
Ed Moncrief, Salinas, CA
Roman Catholic
LeRoy Moreno, Englewood, CO
Assembly of God
Don Mosley, Comer, GA
Ecumenical
Michael Mumma, Lancaster, PA
Presbyterian
John Newell, Dayton, OH
American Baptist
Stephen Nikochik, Narbeth, PA
Roman Catholic
Norman & Sandra Norris,
Barrington, RI
American Baptist
M. Diane Nunnelee, Fayette, MO
United Methodist
Mary Lynn Oglesbee,
Minneapolis, MN
United Methodist
Bob Olsen, State College, PA
Church of the Brethren
Sandy Owen, Austin, TX
Disciples of Christ
Bonnie Payne, Prairie Village, KS
Nondenominational
George Percival, Santa Rosa, CA
United Church of Christ
Jim Perigo, Evansville, IN
United Church of Christ
John M. Perkins, Pasadena, CA
Interdenominational
Sr. Mary Barbara Philippart,
Puno, PERU
Roman Catholic
Michael Potter, Chapel Hill, NC
Roman Catholic

John & Mary Pritchard, Liberty,
MO
Presbyterian
Elvan Ann Putman, Decatur, GA
Baptist
Paul Rader, Huntington, WV
Presbyterian
Robert L. Rader, Ironton, OH
American Baptist
Jim Ranck, Johns Island, SC
Mennonite
Kenneth Rathert, Winter Haven,
FL
Lutheran
Neill Richards, New York, NY
United Church of Christ
Olivia Rojas, Cuauhtemoc,
Chihuahua, MEXICO
Nondenominational
Cammie Rowe, Washington, DC
American Baptist
Al Russell, Houston, TX
Disciples of Christ
Dean Russell, Fayetteville, NC
United Methodist
Quita Russell, Longview, TX
Presbyterian
Audrey Sanders, Portland, OR
Disciples of Christ
William Charles Sanford,
Atwater, CA
United Methodist
Harry Sangree, New York, NY
Presbyterian
Sterling W. Schallert, Madison, WI
American Baptist
James F. Scherfee, Santa Rosa,
CA
United Church of Christ
Thomas Schleifer, Greenville, NC
Roman Catholic

Marilyn Schmalz, Columbus, GA
Seventh-Day Adventist
Mason Schumacher, Boulder, CO
Episcopalian
Wally Scofield, Westport, CT
Presbyterian
Diane Scott, Salem, NJ
American Baptist
Charles Selby, Old Fort, OH
United Methodist
John & Marsha Sellars,
Springfield, MO
Presbyterian
Matthew Shannahan, Dunwoody,
GA
Roman Catholic
Karen Shannahan, Atlanta, GA
Roman Catholic
W.W. Sloan, Burlington, NC
United Church of Christ
Deen Day Smith, Norcross, GA
Southern Baptist
David Spencer, Encino Hills, CA
Nondenominational
John Spencer, John's Island, SC
Episcopalian
John Stahl-Wert, Pittsburgh, PA
Mennonite
Henry King Stanford, Americus,
GA
United Methodist
Ted & Vada Stanley, Westport, CT
Ecumenical
John Staton, Green Bay, WI
United Church of Christ
Robbie Stephens, Oklahoma City,
OK
Southern Baptist
Bernard Strasser, Ormond
Beach, FL
Presbyterian

Christine Street, Marietta, GA
Episcopalian
Charles M. Sutherland, Jr.,
Atlanta, GA
Church of God
Kay Swicord, Brookeville, MD
Presbyterian
Jack Swisher, Covington, KY
Presbyterian
Donald Tarr, Salinas, CA
United Methodist
George N. Theuer, Americus, GA
United Methodist
Joseph Thomas, Milledgeville,
GA
Southern Baptist
Rhodes Thompson, Enid, OK
Disciples of Christ
Leonard L. Tillett, Norwich,
ENGLAND
Congregational
Nancy Tilley, Jackson, TN
Southern Baptist
Franklin Townsend, Lake
Odessa, MI
Church of the Brethren
Charles "Bo" Turner, Clarkesville,
GA
Southern Baptist
Carl Umland, Houston, TX
United Church of Christ
Dolores Van Loucks, Los Gatos,
CA
United Church of Christ
Jack VandenHengel, Baltimore,
MD
Southern Baptist
Carl Walker, Kalamazoo, MI
United Methodist
Charles Warren, Atlanta, GA
Southern Baptist

W. James White, Morristown, NJ
United Methodist
Ralph Whittenburg, South Bend,
IN
Lutheran
Sue Wieland, Atlanta, GA
Presbyterian
Bill Wiley, Jewett, OH
Presbyterian
Robert Wilson, Mooresville, NC
Disciples of Christ

Jack & Lois Wolters, Columbus,
NC
United Church of Christ
Donald & Madonna Yates, Terre
Haute, IN
Presbyterian
Ronald Yates, Acton, MA
United Church of Christ
Jean C. Young, Atlanta, GA
United Church of Christ

Appendix F

International Partners (1973–1990)
(including longer-term volunteers)
(as of April 1, 1990)

Africa:

Gitega, Burundi
Alan Wagman and Anne
   McCormick

Assinman, Ghana
Shirley Buse
Gene Canfield
Wayne Nelson
Felipe Perdomo

Lubokha, Kenya
Kaimentti and Tom
   MacWilliams, Linda and
   Jahmalla

Ndabarnach, Kenya
Michael Harland

Nzoia Community, Kenya
Marjorie Fox
Paul Haddad
Dan Haling
Karen and Mark Lassman-Eul
Hugh O'Brien
Dan and Susan Rhema, Sydel

Lilongwe, Malawi
Dan Haling
Elma and Miles Richmond,
   Paula, Wesley and Micah

Alexandra, South Africa
Helene Friedman

Kasulu, Tanzania
Tim Idle
Dixie and Winston Slider,
   Ambika, Heather and Tekla

Gulu, Uganda
Hulen and Wil Brown
Paul Haddad
Ginny and Jim Handley
Clive Rainey
Joseph Wheeler
Paula Young

Kasese, Uganda
Gloria and Ray Cunningham

Baraka, Zaire
Donna and Mike Thomas,
   Samuel and Michelle

Basankusu, Zaire
Gil Blaisdell
Bill Clifton
Herman and Julienne
   Hymerikx
Erasmus Meinerts
Kathleen Ward

Bikoro, Zaire
Marian Rose

Gemena, Zaire
Barbara and Greg Garrett
Alice Miller
Phil and Pixi Phillips, Kem,
    Christi and Lorenza
Bill Posey
Betsy and Bill Ragan

Ikoko Bonginda, Zaire
R. Dean BeBoer
Larry Hart
Beth and Ken Reno, Melissa

Kikwit, Zaire
Glen and Phyllis Boese, Steve
David and Jan Byerlee,
    Sara Jo
Norma Ueleke Engelhardt
Charlie Forst, Jacquie

Kinshasa, Zaire
Ken Braun
David and Jan Byerlee,
    Sara Jo and Paxton
Chuck Clark
Margee and Mark Frey,
    Matthew and Meredith
Larry Hart
Karen and Larry Karpack
Robbie MacDonald
Art Mehaffey
Clive Rainey
Beth and Ken Reno, Melissa
    and Jonathan
Christian Sheline
Cliff and Joy Stabell
Anne Westman
John Yeatman

Lake Tumba, Zaire
Peggy Bliek
Herman Clausen
R. Dean DeBoer
Laura Freeland

Rex Gardner
Larry Hart
Eula Johnson
Scott Metzel
Marian Rose
Phil Steinkamp
Joe Talento
Bobbie Jo Whitney

Mbandaka, Zaire
Chuck Clark
Pat Clark
Karen Foreman
Dan Froese
Linda and Millard Fuller,
    Chris, Kim, Faith and
    Georgia
Harry and Luanne Goodall
Ken Harris
Alan and Penny Johnson,
    David and Bethany Ann
Joe Kirk
Lobunza and Peter Kratzat,
    Monzoi, Edwin and
    Emmanuel
Martine Lihoreau
Dale Long
Bruce McCrae
Cindy Miller
Roger Miller
Jeff Moger
Don Mosley
Ron Prior
Dan Roman
Harry Sangree
Ken Sauder
Mary Schroeder
David Seely
Christian Sheline
Larry Stoner
Bonnie Watson

207

Ntondo, Zaire
  Jeff Buttram
  Pat Clark
  Peter Clarke
  Bill Clifton
  Beth Corbitt
  Janet Leckrone Corbitt
  Jane and Ralph Gnann, Sidney
    and John
  Karen and Ryan Karis
  Mitch Kjose
  Peter Kratzat
  Ronn Kreps
  Chris and Dodie Lepp, Topher
  Dale Long
  David and Donna Moss,
    Rachel and Laura
  Debbie Pfau
  Beth and Ken Reno, Melissa
  Dan Roman
  Dana Rominger
  Mark Rylance
  Ken Sauder
  Perry Schempp
  Bill and Connie Ward

Chanyanya, Zambia
  Bill Allison
  Bob and Kay Olson
  Mindy and Tim Smith, Diana
    and Christina

Kabuyu Island, Zambia
  Bill Allison
  Lee Chaudoin

Asia:

Bombay, India
  Jack Amick
  John Riley

Hubli, India
  Kathleen Doak

  Jim Mellott
  Tim Swauger

Khammam, India
  Sujatha and Wes Blackstone
  Barbara and Roger Sneller,
    Abbey, Anjuli and Andrew

Koovapally, India
  Sarah Bell
  Maureen Fischer

Islamabad, Pakistan
  Wayne Britt
  Todd Garth

Pacific:

Kusip, Papua New Guinea
  Bryan and Janell Bargen,
    Josiah
  Jeff Lehman
  David and Donna Minich, Julie,
    Jaimie, Jonathan, Joshua
    and Justin
  Mark Sletten

Port Moresby, Papua New Guinea
  Ann and John Franken
  Evelyn and Gordon Lange
  Chris Niebuhr
  John Spratt
  Pat and Russ Wolford, Laura,
    Kathleen and Ryan

Balintocatoc, Philippines
  Bill Allison
  Ruth Pendergrast
  Yvonne Zavithsanos

Dumaguete City, Philippines
  Ellen and Wayne Patton, Jacob

General Santos City, Philippines
  Robert Odum
  Bob Williams

Metro Manila, Philippines
Gai and Mark Case, Glenn,
Lauren and Daniella

Midsayap, Philippines
Louise Nelson

East Fataleka, Solomon Islands
Amy and Nate Pollock

Luma, Solomon Islands
Mary and Neil Essila, Sarah
and Michael

Tepuke, Solomon Islands
Keith and Rona Branson
Michele and Terry Finseth,
Malia and Travis

Latin America/Caribbean:

Alto Beni, Bolivia
Joe Brunet
Larry Godeke
Phineas Gosselink
Steven Robertshaw
Luke Stollings

Belo Horizonte, Brazil
Jim Eustice
Izary Pinto

Esparza, Costa Rica
Bob and Mary
Velasquez-Bertram, Maria,
Albert, Bobby and Joseph
Kay Spofford
Dick Stiefvater

Heredia, Costa Rica
Paul and Terry Simon, Nan
and Paul

Los Cocos, Dominican Republic
Jim Airola
Todd Barto

Rick Simpson
Bruce Yoder

Enriquillo, Dominican Republic
Paul Stoffle

Aguacatan, Guatemala
Diane and Lowell Birkey
Keith Branson
Kitty Brown
Dick Perry
Steve Salsa
Becky and David Sheill
Paul and Terry Simon, Nan
and Paul
Betty Jo and Bob Stevens,
Michelle and Eric

El Rosario, Guatemala
Doug Adams
Evan Lowell
Rob Mercantante

Huehuetenango, Guatemala
Dick Perry
Paul Van Tongeren

San Juan Ixcoy, Guatemala
Barbara Huttman and Thomas
Lamble

San Juan La Laguna, Guatemala
Kitty Brown
Patty and Roger Capron

Dumay, Haiti
Rob DeRocker
Eleanor Frank
Lance and Stephanie
Fryholm-Cheslock
Carl and Pam Hanson, Ian
John Liacos
Robert Lieske
Tim Rockwell
Art Russell

Les Cayes, Haiti
Marie and Tom Dionne,
Zachary, Natali, Rachel,
Matthew and Andrea
Bobbie and Tal Lackey

Pandyassou, Haiti
Bryan and Gail Murphy

Yure River, Honduras
Bob Gronhovd
Daniel A. Lopez

Anahuac, Mexico
Ellen and Fred Schippert

San Pedro Capula, Mexico
Eric Duell
Jerry Fenton

Dexthi Alberto, Mexico
Gayle Gonsior and Larry
Fickbolm, Chelsea and
Lucas

Bluefields, Nicaragua
John and Julia McCray-
Goldsmith

German Pomares, Nicaragua
Susan Bailey
Sarah and Jim Hornsby,
Matthew
Tom Klein
Julie Knop
Cory Scholtes

Jinotega, Nicaragua
Dona and Pat Whitmore-
McDonough
Cathy Miller

Juigalpa, Nicaragua
Rob Massoneau

Managua, Nicaragua
Carole Harper

Matagalpa, Nicaragua
Carole Harper and Mike
Prentiss

Mulukuku, Nicaragua
Jerry Fenton
Brian and Jane Thomas

*Pearl Lagoon/Haulover,
Nicaragua*
Tom Klein

Puertas Viejas, Nicaragua
Lynne and Tim
Barolet-Fogarty, Ryan and
Megan

*Ticuantepe/La Aduana,
Nicaragua*
Anne and Dale Bussis

Arequipa, Peru
Graciella and Jeff Abbott,
Gabriel, Jeffrey and
Jacquelyn

Juliaca, Peru
Debbie and Andy Kramer, Eric,
Wesley, Jessee and
Christen
Peter Shaw
Bret Stein

Manazo, Peru
Ann Bancroft

Puno, Peru
Keith Branson
Elvin Compy, Nick
Susan and Dan Rhema, Sydel
Peter Shaw
Nancy Straus
Chichi and Ken VanDyke, Ross
and Danielle

Long-Term Volunteers in the International Office
(1977–1990)
(who served one year or more)

John Alexander
Alice Anderson
Nancy Anderson
Belinda Angle
Nathan Arndt
Eric Atler
Bob and Joanne Avers
Barbara Baker
Betsy and Skip Baker-Smith,
    Christy and Daniel
Stephen Baker
Beth Balsbaugh
Jean and Walt Bastian
Bill Bates
Gary and Linda Bergh, Susan and
    David
Evelyn and Roy Bickley
Cathy and Jim Binns, Elliott
Gil Blaisdell
Renee Boutin
Kevin Bowers
Nancy and Wallace Braud,
    Hannah and Michael
Bill Brauner
Holly Sawyer Brauner
JoAnn Brenneman
Hulen and Wil Brown
Veronica Brown
Trish Bryan
Phil Buchanan
Kim Budke
Beth Buley
Craig Bunyea
Pat Burdette
Janet and Paul Burger, Marty,
    Ann and Roger
Bill and Joan Burnett
Marvin Burrows

Carolyn Bush
Perry Bush
Albert Campanella
Charles Campbell
Linda Carl
Judi Carpenter
Martha Chandley
Jim Chaney
Lee Chaudoin
Ruth Clark
Nancy Clausen
Bob Clemente
Nick Compy
George and Ruth Comstock
David Conley
Joe and Rose Crowley
Martha Cruz
Ken De Candio
Denise De Lucia
Kathleen Doak
Kathie and Paul DuPont, Jennifer,
    Lisa and Kevin
John Eden
Phil Elwood
Georgia Emory
Dave Enting
Joy Esbenshade
Marilyn Farquhar
Cheryl Fleetwood
RaeAnn Flick
Karen Foreman
Bob and Katherine Foster
Rene Foster
David Fouse
Crystal Frament
Donne and Lynn Frey, Connie,
    Kevin, Karl and Carrie
Linda Fuller

Diane Fulp
Barbara Garvin
Bob and Kathy Geyer, Scott and
   Matthew
Andy and Fran Gibson
Twila Gingrich
Cheryl Gloss
Gerry Glynn
Samuel Gneiting
Michael Good
Gene and Patti Grier
Kenneth Groves
Teri Harris
Donna Hefferman
Elizabeth and Wilbur
   Hershberger, Anna, Maria,
   Sarah and Rachel
Duane and Ruth Hershberger,
   Ben and Heide
Marlene Hess
Charlotte Eby High
Steve High
Sallie Hirst
Geneva Hodges
Dirk and Pam Holkeboer,
   Matthew and Brian
Elizabeth Holler
Cindy Hollinger
Clarence Hollis
Bob and Joyce Hooley-Gingrich
David Hovestol
Phil Hoy
Amy Thomas Huddleston
David Hungerford
Melissa Hurst
Sue Ice
Wesley Ingram
Faye Inlow
Thomas Jackson
David Jones
David and Mary Joseph

Ken and Nancy Keefer,
   Megan and Joshua
Donald Scott Keeler
Cindy Kennedy
Jane Kennedy
Loree Kirk
David Kreider
Aafke Kruizinga
David Landis
David Langdon
Willie Laster
Claudia Ledwich
Cleta Lee
Karl Lempp
Tina Letzelter
Dee and Howard Liebert
Ruth Lindsey
Ann Gunderson Little
Douglas Little
Carolyn and Roland Longenecker,
   Adrienne and Janita
Kika Loucaides
Bob Lucas
Linda MacColl
Robbie MacDonald
Clara Maendel
Sarah and Solomon Maendel,
   Keith, Steve, Karen, Mark,
   Eleanor and Timothy
Steven Marchant
Amy Martel
Steve Martindale
Lloyd and Michelle Mayer
Ray Maynor
Bob and Marion Mayo
David Mayou
Bill McCaffrey
Julia McCray
Carolyn McGarity
Art and Dorothy McIlwain
Ken McKenna

Darryl McMillan
Don Mellinger
Gloria and Noel Miller
Dennis and Vert Miller
Paul and Linda Mills,
    Amy, Ben and John
Len Modeen
Todd Moldenhauer
Amy and Bill Moore
Jim Moyer
Patrick Murphy
Marjorie Musselman
Susan Waldorf Nelson
David Neun
Dwane Newswanger
Don and Faye Nyce
Kaye Noffsinger
Cindy Nolt
Hugh O'Brien
Tim O'Donnell
Bernice Oldham
Jill Ortman
Sue Oths
Richard Owen
Kent Palmer
Joel Palmquist
Amy Parsons
Guy Patrick
Paul Pegler
Richard Pollette
Amy Durkee Pollock
Nate Pollock
Tripp Pomeroy
Tom Powers
Janette Prickett
Ron Prior
Clive Rainey
Luis Re
Sam and Katy Reist, Peter
Brad Rench
Laurie Riggs

Elma Richmond
Dan Riley
Ginny and Johnny Roberts
Vernon Robertson
Susie Roes
Merris Rowe
Greg Sandor
Carol Schlenker
Charlene and Ken Schildt, Mark,
    Laura and Bret
Fred Schippert
Cory Scholtes
Joyce Schwartz
Ray Scioscia
Fran Seaver
Becky and David Sheill, Matthew
Steve Sheridan and Anne Tabor
Rachel and Dan Shinkle
Bev Showalter
Vonnee Sleighter, Jamie
Mark Sloan
Amber Smith
Ashley Smith
Bill Smith
Fiona Smith
Melanie Smith
Melissa Smith
Wylodee Souvie
John Spratt
Donna Stevens
Frank and Janet Stoffle,
    Audrey and Jeffrey
Nancy Straus
Helen Street
Ellen Studley
Joyce Swartz
Judy Szbara
Janet Tadie
Carolyn Ross Talboys
Pete Talboys
Carl Thomas

213

Alice and Gene Tiller
Tom Trainor
Mary and Ora Troyer
Raquel Urroz
Ed Vennell
John Verploegh
Lisa Verploegh
Jeanine Vlasits
Carl Vogel
Roger Vonland
Anita Wallace
Jeff Waltzer
Flo Wanger
Brian Warford
Ed and Mary Warmoth
Bonnie Watson
Brian Weaver
Lynn and Tom Webster, Corey
    and K. C.

Jean Weinhold
Dea Weisenbeck
Sue West
Jack Westfall
Grace Whitlock
Leon Wilburn
Claire Williams
Elizabeth and Tim Wilson
Kim Wilson
Jack and Lois Wolters
Mark Wright
Karl Yoder
Ruth Pendergrast Yoder
Steve Zale
Pamela Zimmerman
Omar Zook

For further information about Habitat for Humanity International, write or call the Regional or National Center nearest you (see list in Appendix B) or the International headquarters:

> Habitat for Humanity International
> Habitat and Church Streets
> Americus, Georgia   31709-3498
> Telephone: (912) 924-6935
> FAX: (912) 924-6541

Videos and earlier books about the ministry of Habitat for Humanity (available at the above address):

How to Start a Habitat for Humanity Affiliate   Helpful, detailed information regarding the steps (philosophical and practical) involved in starting an affiliated Habitat project. (1989)

How-to Workbook   Tells step-by-step how to start a Habitat project in a developing country. Available in English and Spanish. (1990)

No More Shacks!   The continuing story of Habitat for Humanity's growth. Goal stated to eliminate poverty housing by making shelter a matter of conscience. Tells beginning of former President Carter's involvement. By Millard Fuller with Diane Scott. (1986)

Love in the Mortar Joints   The story of Habitat for Humanity's first four years of growth; the launching of sixteen projects in North America, Africa and Central America. By Millard Fuller and Diane Scott. (1980)

Bokotola   Habitat's beginnings as a housing ministry in Mbandaka, Zaire, and the vision of providing decent housing for God's people in need all over the world. By Millard Fuller. (1977)

The Excitement Is Building (video)   Two programs on same videotape: Jimmy Carter Work Projects in Atlanta and Philadelphia in 1988 and House-Raising Walk '88. (1988)

Building a Global Village (video)   Highlights overseas work of Habitat for Humanity. (1989)